DISAPPEARING
AND REVIVING

DISAPPEARING AND REVIVING

Sándor Ferenczi
in the History of Psychoanalysis

André E. Haynal

KARNAC

LONDON   NEW YORK

First published in 2002 by
H. Karnac (Books) Ltd.
6 Pembroke Buildings, London NW10 6RE

A subsidiary of Other Press LLC, New York

British Library Cataloguing in Publication Data

A C.I.P. for this book is available from the British Library

ISBN 1 85575 254 9

10 9 8 7 6 5 4 3 2 1

Edited, designed, and produced by Communication Crafts

www.karnacbooks.com

Printed and bound by Antony Rowe Ltd, Eastbourne

To Véronique,
Cleo, and David

CONTENTS

ACKNOWLEDGEMENTS

Acknowledgement is gratefully made to the following journals and book publishers for permission to reprint parts of chapters or entire chapters in this volume:

Chapter 2 was originally published in *Free Associations*, London, 2/1 (21): 1–20, 1991.

Chapter 3 was originally published in *Journal of the American Academy of Psychoanalysis*, 21 (1993, 4): 605–621.

Chapter 4 was originally published in *International Review of Psycho-Analysis*, 16 (1989, 3): 315–321.

Chapter 6 was originally published in *Psychoanalytic Inquiry*, 13 (1993, 4): 355–371.

Chapter 8 was originally published in L. M. Hermanns (Ed.), *Spaltungen in der Geschichte der Psychoanalyse* (pp. 94–105). Tübingen: Diskord, 1995.

Chapter 2 was translated from French into English by Ruth Ward, and chapters 1, 5, and 7 by Philip Slotkin, MA Cantab. MITI.

Grateful acknowledgment is made to Judith Dupont for her permission to quote from Sándor Ferenczi's *First Contributions to Psycho-Analysis, Further Contributions to the Theory and Technique of Psycho-Analysis,* and *Final Contributions to the Problems and Methods of Psycho-Analysis.*

Thanks are also due to the Harvard University Press for excerpts reprinted by perission of the publisher from *The Clinical Diary of Sandor Ferenczi,* edited by Judith Dupot, translated by Michael Balint and Nicola Zarday Jackson (Cambridge, Mass.: Harvard University Press), Copyright © 1985 by Payot, Paris, by arrangement with Mark Paterson, Copyright 1988 by Nicola Jackson for English translation.

PREFACE

This book is, in a way, a continuation of my former volume, *The Technique at Issue, Controversies in Psychoanalysis: From Freud and Ferenczi to Michael Balint* (Karnac Books, London, 1988), which was centred on the work of Michael Balint, his forerunners (Ferenczi and the Budapest school), and his descendants. My present contribution hopes to settle a debt I feel I owe to Ferenczi—the founder of all relationship-based psychoanalysis and the explorer of traumatism, countertransference, as well as other problems important for contemporary psychoanalysis.

To write a piece of the complex history of psychoanalysis by drawing a picture of one of the pioneers of this practice and science means to have a dialogue with this character, to ask him questions—today's questions, of course—and to see what he answers. In this sense, this book is not detached from our contemporary practice and theoretical controversies. It tries to be a faithful reflection of what Ferenczi proposed for the still very present problems of psychoanalytic practice and theory.

Besides, as my text reflects questions and preoccupations more than twenty years old, based on historical sources such as letters, notes, published books, and works of students and contradictors, this book is also a memory of thoughts and queries stretching over several decades.

It is also the commemoration of an intense collaboration with two people who walked through my intellectual and clinical adventures. Both are bound to this book as kinds of co-authors. The first is Ernst Falzeder, Ph.D., co-author of articles that were used as basic material for chapters 2, 3, and 6. Ernst and I have elaborated the "project Ferenczi", part of which was the editing of the correspondence between Ferenczi and Freud. My other faithful assistant is Maud Struchen, who has been working with me for almost thirty years; I owe her the quality of the French text and the precision of the bibliography. Years of collaboration with these two people stay unforgettable in my life, and for this they are deeply and personally thanked. My heartfelt thanks go to Klara King for her thorough editorial work. I am also indebted to Véronique Haynal-Reymond for her untiring help she provided me throughout the entire preparation of this book.

ABBREVIATIONS

Abr	Karl Abraham	Grod	Georg Groddeck
AS	Lou Andreas-Salomé	Ju	Carl Gustav Jung
Bal	Michael Balint	Jo	Ernest Jones
Bins	Ludwig Binswanger	Pf	Oscar Pfister
Eit	Max Eitingon	R	Otto Rank
F	Sigmund Freud	Sa	Hanns Sachs
Fer	Sándor Ferenczi	SZw	Stefan Zweig
Fl	Wilhelm Fliess		

Correspondence is shown in the form: "Abr/F" (Abraham to Freud), etc.

The references to the work of Ferenczi follow the bibliography of the author established by Balint; the figures in square brackets refer to Balint's list of Ferenczi's works in S. Ferenczi, *Schriften zur Psychoanalyse* (2 vols., Frankfurt/Main, Fischer, 1970, 1972). The works of Michael Balint are quoted according to the bibliography published in Haynal, *The Technique at Issue* (London: Karnac Books, 1988).

DISAPPEARING
AND REVIVING

CHAPTER ONE

Ferenczi:
a "pre"-psychoanalyst?

A convenient distinction: everything in Ferenczi's career *before* he met Freud in 1908 was *pre*psychoanalytic, and everything that came after was . . . psychoanalytic. Three months after the first conversation between the two men, Ferenczi was addressing the Salzburg Congress. Had he become a psychoanalyst in three months? That would be a record even for Ferenczi! The truth is plainly more complex.

The epic history of the Ferenczi family is typical of that of a particular section of the Budapest intelligentsia. The father, Baruch Fraenkel, was born in Cracow in 1830; he emigrated from Galicia, a province in the Austrian part of the Austro–Hungarian Empire, to northern Hungary and settled in Miskolc. Caught up in the early-nineteenth-century liberal–nationalist movement, he became so involved in this that he had his name Magyarized to Bernát (Bernard) Ferenczi when Sándor was six years old. He owned a bookshop and a publishing house. After the 1848 liberal and nationalist revolution, which broke over Hungary as it did over most of the countries of Europe, and its subsequent defeat he became the printer for an entire vein of Hungarian progressive literature.

Interestingly, the works issuing from his press included those of a Protestant pastor from a nearby village, Mihály Tompa. During the years of repression pending the reconciliation between the House of Habsburg and the Hungarian nation in 1867, Ferenczi the elder was one of those who kept these cultural ideals aloft.

Sándor's mother, Roza Eibenschütz, had been brought up in Vienna (in German), so that the family was bilingual, if not indeed multilingual (speaking German, Hungarian, Polish, and possibly Yiddish).

Ferenczi himself, the eighth of eleven children growing up in this middle-class setting, was an early developer who "played" with hypnosis while still at the *"Gymnasium"* [high school]. As a student at the Vienna Medical School, he was exposed to influences such as the Darwinism of his teacher, Claus, the physiology of Brücke, the philosophy of Mach, and the sexology of Krafft-Ebing—the seething mass of cultures that burst onto the scene—so inexplicably, from our present-day vantage point—in the dying days of the nineteenth century in Vienna, and which Ferenczi was to rediscover shortly afterwards in Budapest, where he moved on completing his studies.

Hungary's capital city of Budapest was created in 1872 with the union of Buda—the district of the Royal Palace—and Pest, a town of merchants, small craftsmen, the university, and broad boulevards with those famous cafés where ideas and influences were exchanged between intellectuals, journalists, poets, and novelists—circles in which Ferenczi, too, moved. These twin towns were to share second and third place in the Austro–Hungarian Empire after Prague. That intelligentsia, which was as remote from provincial Hungary as Paris's Left Bank is from rural France, consisted largely of émigrés from the different lands of the monarchy: German-speakers from the relevant regions of the Empire; Jews from western Poland, and Hungarian-speakers from distant provinces such as the Principality of Transylvania (now Western Romania). The prevailing mixture of languages and cultures was typically Central European. The philosopher Georg Lukács, later to become a Marxist, and Béla Balázs, the librettist of two of Bartók's most famous works (*The Wooden Prince* and *Bluebeard's Castle*), are good examples: Lukács wrote most of his works in German, whereas for Balázs the language was now German, now Hungarian. Sándor

Ferenczi set down his *Clinical Diary* in German! Even if the nationalists ultimately caused the Empire to burst asunder—through the Treaty of Versailles after the First World War—the cosmopolitan culture of the major cities of central Europe was to impress its stamp deeply on twentieth-century culture in general, through its expatriate geniuses and talents such as—to name but a few— Freud in London, Wittgenstein in Cambridge, and Schoenberg in California.

After his studies in Vienna, Ferenczi settled in Budapest, which subsequently proved particularly fertile soil for psychoanalysis to take root in. It may be that this culture had less affinity for highly abstract thought—specifically, philosophy—than for fields such as music, painting, and, by virtue of its links with the Vienna Medical School, therapeutic action (e.g. Semmelweis). As it happens, the Budapest Medical School worked closely together with its Viennese counterpart, which, we may recall, was at the time itself vying with those of Paris, London, and some of the fast-expanding German universities. It practised new methods of auscultation and percussion, an anatomical pathology (Rokitansky), and a modern physiology (whose leading light was Brücke, a member of Helmholtz's famous circle, which sought to place physiology on a physical and chemical basis). Darwinian thought was represented there through Claus; and it was the seat of nascent sciences such as sexology and psychiatry.

Occultism

Back in Budapest after his Viennese training in 1899, Ferenczi worked first as an extern at one of Budapest's oldest hospitals, Rókus-Kórház—one of those venerable institutions (to be more precise, the hospital was in Pest, the town of merchants and the middle classes, as opposed to Buda, the right-bank district, containing the Royal Palace and bourgeois villas). He then practised in a clinic for the poor of the city called Erzsébet Szegényház, and later in an insurance outpatient clinic for blue-collar workers. Lastly, he worked in the same Rókus-Kórház for a very authoritative and malignant Chief—"a hard-hearted man", as Ferenczi described him (Ferenczi, 1917 [199], p. 288)—who had Ferenczi take care of the prostitutes instead of letting him devote his time to the study of psychic phenomena. In the absence of other material, he attempted psychology experiments on himself by the method of "automatic writing" (Ferenczi, 1917 [199], p. 288)—that is, free associations in writing, quite widely used at this time, and of which spiritualists often spoke. It was already a kind of auto-analysis. At the same time, in Vienna, what has come to be known as Freud's "self-analysis" was taking place; this too, it will be recalled, involved the writing down of dreams and their associations (Mahony, 1993). Much later, as it happens, in a letter to her father dated 7 August 1921, Anna Freud was to comment: "Now at last I also believe you when you say that dream analyses, if made by oneself, can only be done in writing" ["Jetzt endlich glaube ich Dir auch, daß man die Traumanalysen, wenn man sie allein macht, nur schriftlich machen kann"—Grubrich-Simitis, 1993, p. 79, n. 13].

Just as Freud had had his friend Fliess, so Ferenczi's friendship with Freud was preceded by his association with Miksa Schächter, a distinguished and cultivated physician and editor of the famous Hungarian progressive medical journal Gyógyászat [Therapy]. Schächter was a kind of paternal friend: here Ferenczi can already be seen seeking an idealized father as an interlocutor for his self-analysis, the same role that he later expected Freud to fulfil: "I wanted to enjoy the man, not the scholar, in close friendship" (Fer/F, 3.10.1910).

By the turn of the century, Ferenczi had already read Freud and Breuer's paper "On the Psychical Mechanism of Hysterical Phenomena" ["Über den psychischen Mechanismus hysterischer Phänomene", 1893h, which had been published in the Wiener medizinische Presse]; he commented that it had at the time appeared to him "improbable and artificial", and subsequently he blamed himself for not having "honour[ed] it with a closer scrutiny" (Ferenczi, 1908 [60], p. 31). As a medical student in Vienna, he had already attended the courses given by Krafft-Ebing, author of the celebrated Psychopathia Sexualis (1886) and father of the terms "sadism" and "masochism", who had, as it happened, annoyed him with his ironic remarks about hypnosis. Ferenczi had, of course, spent his student years in the Vienna of Klimt, the great artist of erotism, of

Schnitzler, who wrote about problems of sexuality, illusion, and reality, of Rilke, and of Hofmannsthal, before returning in 1897 to the Budapest of Ignotus, Dezsö Kosztolányi, and Géza Csáth. The passion for exploring the secrets of the human psyche by free association, then very much in vogue in psychology, belonged to the common cultural background of the two men who shared the initials S.F. Coupled with Ferenczi's reading of *The Interpretation of Dreams* at the beginning of the century, this research led him to approach Jung. After a brief visit to Vienna in March 1907—where he met Freud on the 3rd and participated in a meeting of the "Wednesday Society" on the 6th—Jung spent a few days in Budapest with Ferenczi's friend and colleague, Dr Fülöp Stein, who was in touch with Jung on account of their common interest in alcoholism and the temperance movement. It was on this occasion that they met for the first time. Later that year, still pushed by his interests for the word-association method, Ferenczi spent a short period at the Burghölzli Clinic in Zurich (unpublished letter from Jung to Ferenczi dated 1.10.1907; cf. Freud/Ferenczi, 1993, p. 2, n. 4). Everyone around him was subjected to experiments in which he used a stopwatch to measure the time elapsing between the stimulus word and the response; not even the lavatory attendant at the Café Royal, where he was a regular, was spared (Balint, 1964g). (In fact, Jung had written *Studies in Word Association*, published between 1904 and 1907, one chapter of which, "Psychoanalysis and Association Experiments", he sent to Freud with a view to making contact with him.)

Whereas Freud saw himself as belonging within the line of descent begun with mesmerism in France, which became the hypnotism of Charcot and Bernheim, Ferenczi was *in addition*, close to *another* cultural tradition of the mysterious—namely, *occultism*. Characteristically, he mentions this in connection with automatic writing ("about which the spiritualists have much to say"—Ferenczi, 1917 [199], p. 288). And it was spiritualism that led to his own initial discovery of the *unconscious* and of the existence of splits in the psyche. While this may not be particularly surprising at a time when hysteria and multiple personalities were all the rage, the link forged by Ferenczi is highly original: "What we know today proves beyond a shadow of doubt that there are many unconscious

[*öntudatlan*] and semiconscious elements in psychic functioning."
He therefore considered it "probable that most of the phenomena
of spiritualism are based on the division of the psychic functions
into two or more parts, only one of which is placed at the focus of
the convex mirror of consciousness, whereas the others operate
autonomously outside consciousness [*öntudat nélkül*]. That perhaps
explains how a medium can conduct [his experiments] outside of
his consciousness and not intentionally" (Ferenczi, 1899, p. 478).

The achievement of a better understanding of one of the last
secrets of human communication, nicely expressed through the
word "occult", was long to remain an object of Ferenczi's burning
curiosity, and eventually he was to draw Freud into his wake. Both
men later hoped that the *countertransference* would give up its
secrets through thought transmission. The introduction to the first
volume of the Freud–Ferenczi correspondence (Haynal, 1992a, in
particular p. xxvii ff) tells part of this story and gives an account of
the journey that Freud, Ferenczi, and Jung made to America in
August 1909. Note that this trip came within less than a year of
Ferenczi's making Freud's acquaintance through Jung—that is to
say, *very shortly* after "Ferenczi the psychoanalyst" first took
the stage. The *Correspondence* (Freud/Ferenczi, 1993—for example:
Fer/F, 5.10.1909, Fer/F, 20.11.1909, and, in particular, F/Fer,
6.10.1909; F/Fer, 11.10.1909; F/Fer, 22.10.1909; F/Fer, 10.11.1909)
bears witness to the intensity of the exchanges between Ferenczi
and his master on this subject, as well as to the fact that Ferenczi
was also experimenting with his patients; furthermore it illustrates
the role of Freud's enthusiasm here: "*The transference of your*
thoughts in incomprehensible ways is the strange thing" (emphasis
in original); then follows the characteristic comment: "Keep quiet
about it for the time being" (F/Fer, 6.10.1909). Here the lines of
transfer merge with those of mysteries of occultism, still in the hope
that "*Gedankenübertragung*" [thought-transference] would shed
light on the "*Übertragung*" [transference]. Ferenczi, zealous as always, chased clairvoyants and pythonesses across Europe. Freud
participated in these experiences, played mediums in turn, and
continued this game for many more years. As late as 1925, Freud
wrote to Abraham that Anna had a "telepathic sensitivity" (F/Abr,
9.7.1925). The aim of all this for Freud was "to shatter the doubts
about the existence of thought transference . . . that is where the

doubt ends." However, "preserving the secret long enough" was also an important consideration (F/Fer, 20.8.1910).

Freud, as it happens, never completely lost interest in this subject. At the famous meeting of the "Secret Committee" in the Harz Mountains in 1921, he divulged his ideas on psychoanalysis and telepathy (cf. Freud, 1941d [1921]) to his closest circle of initiates. A year later he was supposed to address the Vienna Psychoanalytic Society on the subject of dreams and telepathy, but for some mysterious reason the lecture was never delivered, although its text was published in *Imago* (Freud, 1922a). Again, in 1922, he wrote to Eitingon that there were two "themes that always perplexed him to distraction" (13.11.1922, quoted by Jones, 1957, p. 419): one was occultism and the other . . . the true identity of the author of Shakespeare's works.

It is hardly necessary to point out that, through the caricature of occultism, Freud and Ferenczi were studying problems that manifestly had to do with *relationship* and *intersubjectivity*, of which the *pre*psychoanalytic Ferenczi was already a master. It is no coincidence that he succeeded, as early as in 1909, in linking the transference to introjection (Ferenczi, 1909 [67]), the latter being understood in a sense that anticipated the projective identification of Melanie Klein (1946a): "I *project* the stimulus words *Ucs.*, he *introjects* them" (Fer/F, 17.8.1910, emphasis in original).

* * *

In 1906 Freud was grappling with the affective implications of the analytic process and the associated transference and countertransference problems. He wrote Jung on 6 December: "Essentially, one might say, the cure is effected by love." A month later, on 30 January 1907, a similar statement appears in the Minutes of the Vienna Psychoanalytic Society: "Our cures are cures of love" (Nunberg & Federn, 1962, p. 101).

He was greatly fired up by this subject. He had already written up the case history of Dora (Freud, 1905e [1901]), set down in one continuous burst of impassioned enthusiasm between 10 and 25 January, interrupting his work on *The Psychopathology of Everyday Life* (Freud, 1901b) for the purpose. At the Salzburg Congress held at Easter, 1908, the first such meeting attended by Ferenczi, Freud was inspired by a similar flame as he presented the analysis of the

Rat Man (Freud, 1909d). He spoke without a break for nearly five hours, impelled by the need to express himself and spurred on by the eager demands of his audience. He manifestly *needed* to free himself, as he disclosed to Abraham three years later, on 3 July 1912: "I have to recuperate from psycho-analysis by working, otherwise I should not be able to stand it" (F/Abr, 3.7.1912); he made a similar comment to Ferenczi at about the same time: "I was depressed the whole time and anesthetized myself with writing—writing—writing" (F/Fer, 2.1.1912).

The inevitable affective *involvement* of the analyst was becoming obvious, and it was the subject of close scrutiny in the Freud–Jung correspondence after Jung's "affair" with Sabina Spielrein: "To be slandered and scorched by the love with which we operate—such are the perils of our trade, which we are certainly not going to abandon on their account." Again: "In league with the Devil and yet you fear fire?" (F/Ju, 9.3.1909). And, once more, to Jung: "Such experiences, though painful, are necessary and hard to avoid. . . . I myself have never been taken in quite so badly, but I have come very close to it a number of times and had *a narrow escape*. . . . But no lasting harm is done. They help us to develop the thick skin we need to dominate 'countertransference' . . . ; they teach us to displace our own affects to best advantage. They are a *blessing in disguise*" (F/Ju, 7.6.1909; both italicized phrases in English in original).

At this stage, Freud and Ferenczi were working *together* to a much greater extent than is generally realized. For instance, when Freud was writing *Totem and Taboo* (1912–13a), Ferenczi reacted immediately (Fer/F, 23.6.1913) by taking up one of his ideas on the transmission of "mental processes. . . . For psycho-analysis has shown us that everyone possesses in his unconscious mental activity an apparatus which enables him to interpret other people's reactions, that is, to undo the distortions which in other people have imposed on the expression of their feelings" (Freud, 1912–13a, p. 159; the original German word, *Gefühlsregungen* [GW IX, p. 191], implies spontaneously arising feelings). In Freud's view, these important communications acted "without passing through the Cs." because "the Ucs. of one human being can react upon that of another" (Freud, 1915e, p. 194).

Again, in a kind of antithesis bequeathed to us by the history of psychoanalysis—a pair of opposites such as Goethe and Schiller, or Plato and Aristotle, as if the human mind needed a good figure and a bad figure even in these fields—some seek to clothe Ferenczi in the *aspects of Freud* they would rather get rid of in order to preserve their idealization unblemished. For instance, many of those who have espoused the biological idea by way of Ferenczi's "Thalassa" are unaware that this was the "Lamarckian" contribution long planned by Freud and himself, which Freud urged Ferenczi to publish. The same applies to many other therapeutic practices: for example, the setting of a time limit for an analysis, which was likewise originally an idea of Freud's. Ferenczi thus played an active part, but Freud was the originator.

Sexuality

Ferenczi's interest in *sexuality* emerged early on, again before he met Freud and immersed himself in his thought. In his paper "A szerelem a tudományban" ["Love in the sciences"] (Ferenczi, 1901), he notes that "sexual love releases immense psychic energies, whose destructive and constructive operation displays the individual and the species at the apex of their capacity to act" (French edition, p. 190). ("Sexual love" is expressed in Hungarian by a single word, *szerelem*, as opposed to *szeretet*, which means love pure and simple, especially from the affective point of view; the two form a pair of opposites like *Eros* and *Agape*.) Like Freud for his part later (for instance: *"what poets and students of human nature had always asserted turned out to be true"*—Freud, 1925d [1924], p. 33), he contends that "even today the only sources of the psychology of love are poetry and the literature of fiction" (p. 191). He links love with possessiveness, the masochistic love of the "uncomprehended" person and his jealousy—the regressive states that may "threaten the individual with psychosis, dissolution, criminality, or addiction to the bottle" (p. 192). The biography of Rozá K (Ferenczi, 1902)—"a veritable odyssey" that has already fascinated a number of authors, such as Lorin (1983) and Rachman (1993)—is substantially based on an autobiography composed at Ferenczi's request by this lesbian transvestite patient. The paper movingly combines classical "anamnesis" with listening to the subjectivity of this marginalized person who had been expelled from Vienna and was living in Budapest; the interest evinced in Rozá K's experience and the capacity for identification are truly characteristic of Ferenczi the therapist. On reading the case history itself, one is indeed impressed by Ferenczi's subtle ability to identify with this unhappy woman, as well as by his attempt, even at the risk of speculation, to introduce a degree of intelligibility into her story. In this article, as well as in his activity in favour of homosexuals, Ferenczi showed how sensitive he was to the necessity of fighting against social repression and to the role physicians, particularly psychiatrists like himself, should play in this battle.

The child

We are admittedly still short of Freud's infantile sexuality of 1905. Yet there are already signs of an interest in the child in the adult, which was to be a consistent element in Ferenczi's lifelong preoccupation with the "wise baby"—as he was later to describe himself when trying to understand the baby in ourselves (Haynal, 1992b). This research was to induce him to elucidate his own countertransference, or indeed trauma, to which he refers in his *Clinical Diary* (Ferenczi, 1985 [1932]), which also led to his final works, such as "Child-Analysis in the Analysis of Adults" (1931 [292] and "Confusion of Tongues between Adults and the Child" (1933 [294]). The foundations were laid very early on, as witness his statement to Freud that children did not need indirect language and hence symbolism [for instance, Fer/F, 1.6.1911, 3.6.1911: *"why children don't understand symbolism (they don't need any yet)"*]. Shortly after their first encounter, Jung invited Ferenczi to give a lecture at the Psychoanalytic Congress in Salzburg. Inspired by Freudian ideas, he talked about "the child", opening new perspectives in child education (Ferenczi, 1908 [63]). As a matter of fact, Ferenczi had always had a deep relation—projective and introjective, I would say a "projective identification"—with the child and even with the baby, and he saw himself as a "wise baby". Some of Ferenczi's readers, misunderstanding him on this point, have accused him of angelism—that is, as it were, of denying infantile sexuality—whereas he was manifestly referring solely to a certain authenticity on the part of children and to environmental pressures in the genesis of repression and "indirect language". His passionate interest in children is reflected in the story of little Árpád (Ferenczi, 1913 [114]) and his constant encouragement of his associates, from Melanie Klein to Alice Balint and Margaret Mahler, to understand children better.

Ferenczi, who saw himself as the *"wise baby"* or *"enfant terrible"* of psychoanalysis, at the same time suffered from this position of identification with the child in his relations with Freud, toward whom he was unable to assert himself (except perhaps at the end of his life). His childhood sufferings, or "trauma", are reflected in his *Clinical Diary*. He tried to understand what "really" happens with a child. Whereas Freud complained to Fliess that Annerl's (little Anna's) *Kinderstube* was closed to him because the womenfolk ["*die Weiblichkeit*"] would not support his researches (F/Fl, 8.2.1897, in Masson, 1985), Ferenczi, for his part, insisted that he wanted not a fantasy child but a real one (Fer/Grod, 1982, p. 60). However, fate (that is, of course, his inner fate) prevented him. . . . Yet the subject itself held him in thrall to the end of his days. It even influenced his choice between Gizella and Elma, as we will see later.

Experimentation

Ferenczi, who had been "practising" hypnosis and writing poems since the age of 16, quickly became an experimenter in the therapeutic situation. While Freud sought to create a situation close to his scientific ideals, whereby objective data originating from the patient could be observed without the "suggestion" of the therapist (e.g. Freud, 1909b, p. 102 passim), Ferenczi from the start had a taste for experimentation; he in fact began—as did Freud himself—by resorting even to the use of electricity (Ferenczi, 1904a), later moving on to hypnosis (Ferenczi, 1904b). Traces of his concern with the latter may be discerned both in his research on the activity of the analyst in the 1920s and in his understanding of deep regressive states.

He regales us from an early date with a number of miniature clinical jewels, published over the ensuing years: he shows, in particular in "Transitory Symptom-Constructions during the Analysis" (Ferenczi, 1912 [85]) and "To Whom Does One Recount One's Dreams?" (Ferenczi, 1913 [105]), how the phenomena of psychoanalytic treatment are conditioned by the transference and countertransference; and a little later he presents already astonishing vistas of various kinds of experiments in analytic therapy (e.g. "Discontinuous Analysis", Ferenczi, 1914 [147]).

Conclusion

Whereas Freud belonged to the B'nai B'rith, Ferenczi was a member of a more secular group, which published *Nyugat* [*The West*]—a very progressive literary and social-science journal whose editor, Hugo Ignotus, was an important literary figure (on the café scene) and one of the founder members—as Ferenczi was wont to say ironically, "*the* member", since the others constituted the Committee—of the Hungarian Psychoanalytic Society, which was established by Ferenczi in 1913 (cf. Jones, 1955, p. 116).

It has been pointed out that, as early as in his 1902 paper on Rozá K, Ferenczi showed himself to be alive to the need to fight social repression, for instance of homosexuality, and to the role of the physician, and in particular the psychiatrist, in this struggle.

* * *

Let us return to the question raised in the title and at the beginning of this chapter: "Was Ferenczi 'pre'-psychoanalytic?" It presupposes a conceptualization like that of stage-by-stage child development—a view that is outmoded, obsolete, and artificial. In the case of Ferenczi, too, we observe a *gradual* development, an originality that seizes upon precise themes from the beginning and delves ever deeper into them, with Ferenczi initially in isolation, substantially ignorant of Freud's work, and then interacting closely with him, as illustrated particularly by the first two volumes of their correspondence. At any rate, Althusser's theory of "epistemological discontinuity"—whereby he places a caesura between the young Marx and the more mature Marx, and which others have sought to apply to the understanding of Freud's *œuvre*—is lame indeed. There is just as much continuity as there are developmental steps—not only a discontinuity, but also a thread that is never cut. This is as true of Freud as it is of Ferenczi, whom we find making Freud's acquaintance when he was already a highly developed technical experimenter and theoretician in his own right. His warm reception by Freud, coupled with the latter's expectations of him, as illustrated by their correspondence, was due to the fact that from the beginning Ferenczi made a contribution of his own. Freud would, moreover, have liked to have him as a partner: "I would have wished for you to . . . take your place next to me as a companion with equal rights, which you did not succeed in doing" (F/Fer, 2.10.1910). Ferenczi was in fact prevented from assuming that place by unconscious hopes that burdened the relationship between the two men—and continued to do so until the end. But rather than run ahead of ourselves, let us merely stress the *continuity* in Ferenczi's *œuvre*—as indeed in Freud's—as a result of which the addition of the prefix "pre-" to "psychoanalytic" does indeed become questionable.

The distance between the two men was not negligible, even at the beginning, considering the differences in their personalities, their interests, and indeed their profound motivations. Some of the themes that Ferenczi was to develop later surely arose out of the frustration of his relationship with Freud, which he wanted to be analytic. From this point of view, some themes are admittedly connected with this partially failed analysis: that of love, the possibility of being analysed to the very end, and the associated ambitions. When Ferenczi expresses his intense desire to be able to tell the truth—"Not everything that is infantile should be abhorred, for example the child's urge for truth . . ." (Fer/F, 12.10.1910)—we may discern his implicit wish for *his* truth, too, to be accepted by the other, who, in this case, was Freud.

All the same, it is also clear that this therapeutic zeal was present from the outset, for example in the pleasure of relationship: Ferenczi was predestined to be one of the *fundamental* artisans of the psychoanalytic relationship and psychoanalytic practice, as, incidentally, Freud had intended (F/Fer, 28.1.1912).

So is Ferenczi's *œuvre* psychoanalytic or not? What we hear is certainly a new tone alongside Freud. But is it psychoanalysis? If, as some hold, psychoanalysis is the work of just one man—Freud— then by definition it is not. However, if it is considered that, in the shadow of a genius, psychoanalysis and its practice were born of the interaction of a number of exceptional people, then Ferenczi certainly has his place too. Freud, after all, was to write that Ferenczi's works "have made all analysts into his pupils" (Freud, 1933c, p. 228)—and also that a "number of papers that appeared later in the literature under his or my name took their first shape in our talks" (p. 227). Ferenczi had already made the point: "Our work should certainly also be called a 'collective' one; each of us must renounce a portion of the satisfaction of our ambition" (Fer/ F, 4.6.1914).

CHAPTER TWO

"Healing through love"?
A unique dialogue
in the history of psychoanalysis

It is true that whenever a crisis broke out Freud invariably showed himself what he really was, a truly great man, who was always accessible and tolerant to new ideas, who was always willing to stop, think anew, even if it meant re-examining even his most basic concepts, in order to find a possibility for understanding what might be valuable in any new idea. It has never been asked whether something in Freud has or has not contributed to a critical increase of tension during the period preceding a crisis. Still less has any analyst bothered to find out what happened in the minds of those who came into conflict with Freud and what in their relationship to him and to psychoanalysis led to the exacerbation. We have been content to describe them as the villains of the piece. . . . Maybe Rank's case is less suitable for this examination but I am quite certain in Ferenczi's case one could follow the development which, prompted by the characters of the two protagonists, led to the tragic conflict . . . (letter from Michael Balint to Ernest Jones, 31.5.57, Balint Archives, Geneva)

I

The relationship between Sigmund Freud and Sándor Ferenczi is described as a controversial dialogue about central subjects in psychoanalysis, the repression of which has had negative effects upon the development of psychoanalysis. Their dialogue about personal and scientific topics, their use of the analytic method in intimate relationships and the effects of these upon their practice and theory are considered in detail. The authors refer partly to some still unpublished material and to Ferenczi's *Clinical Diary*. Consequences of this dialogue are drawn for the present situation in psychoanalysis.

Right up to the present day, the relationship between Freud and Ferenczi has been a difficult topic for psychoanalysis. On the one hand this is understandable, since they themselves had difficulty in coming to an agreement over important theoretical and practical questions such as about the nature of trauma, the relationship between inner and outer reality, the problem of granting or refusing (and how much) satisfaction in therapy, transference and countertransference, and the nature of infantile sexuality. On the other hand, a reluctance to investigate this relationship and these questions without prejudice has disturbed further developments in theory and practice and left the field open to "commercial travellers" (F/Fer, 8.7.1912) (may be expressed as "over-zealous salesmen" for the history of this expression see Haynal (1987, p. 54) and to people who wanted to set up for themselves "with a cannon of their own".[1]

Both have led to a tendency to make a complete split between Freud's and Ferenczi's positions, to identify with one and declare the other wrong, dangerous, or even mad. How far from the truth such a division is can be seen from the fact that the two protago-

---

[1] Reference to one of Freud's favourite stories—e.g. "Itzig had been declared fit for service in the artillery. He was clearly an intelligent lad, but intractable and without any interest in the service. One of his superior officers, who was friendly disposed to him, took him to one side and said to him: 'Itzig, you're no use to us. I'll give you a piece of advice: buy yourself a cannon and make yourself independent!'" (Freud, 1905c, p. 56). Freud was attracted to intractable and intelligent people, if they were interested in service in his "wild army" (Groddeck, 1974, p. 14).

nists themselves never took up such clearly defined positions as are often attributed to them. Even today, the problems they discussed open up important—in fact, basic—questions of psychoanalytic practice and theory. As is well known there were other conflicts between Freud and Ferenczi that were deep-rooted and tragic enough. It is more fruitful not to try to reconcile their attitudes prematurely—that also would not do this controversial dialogue justice.

It was a *dialogue*, it was friendship, more, it was an "intimate sharing of life, feelings and interests" (F/Fer, 11.1.1933). In the scientific field they constantly reported their ideas and projects. Their mutual influence continued beyond estrangement and death. Ferenczi's *Clinical Diary* (1985 [1932]), the product of "immersion in a kind of scientific fantasy and truth" (Fer/F, 1.5.1932), may be read as a letter to Freud. A quarter of a century after Ferenczi's fragment of analysis with him, Freud was still concerned with the question of whether he, Freud, had behaved correctly (Freud, 1937c). One of Freud's last notes, concerning "The splitting of the ego in the process of defence" (1940a [1938]), in which he wrote that he did not know "whether what he wanted to say should be regarded as something long familiar and obvious, or as something entirely new and puzzling" (p. 275), concerned a subject that had been central to Ferenczi's work in later years (Ferenczi, 1938 [1920–32] [308]; 1985 [1932], etc.).

Freud's influence on Ferenczi's work is relatively clear. Letters and Ferenczi's *Diary* clearly show the extent to which he always wrote for Freud (cf. Fer/F, 23.5.1919, 15.5.1922, 30.1.1924), how he discussed the content, timing, and placing of each publication with Freud, and how closely bound up with this relationship his technical experiments were (see below). It is less well known that the ideas in his main work, *A Theory of Genitality* (Ferenczi, 1924 [268]), were the subject of intensive discussion between him and Freud long before this was published, and that there was even a plan to write a "Lamarck-work" together (Fer/F, 2.1.1917).

Freud's way of using other people's ideas was variable. Although he took up other authors' ideas, he worked them over and digested them until such time as they resurfaced as his own. "I . . . tend strongly towards plagiarism", he wrote to Ferenczi (F/Fer, 8.2.1910). And thus many of Ferenczi's ideas and concepts reappear in Freud's work, often after a long period of latency and integrated into his own ideas: thoughts about homosexuality, phylogenesis, trauma, transference and countertransference, ego-development, technique, parapsychology . . .

In addition to the scientific, there was the complicated and deep-rooted personal relationship: Freud's plan for a marriage between his daughter Mathilde and Ferenczi; the journey to America, which they undertook together with Jung; the many joint holidays, with concomitant pleasures and difficulties; Ferenczi's "attempt of an analysis" (F/Fer, 16.11.1916) with Freud; Ferenczi's relationship to his future wife Frau Gizella and her daughter Elma, in which Freud was involved in various ways, including his analysis of Elma; Ferenczi's and Freud's relationships to other analysts, which also had their role in the history of conflict within psychoanalysis: to Jung, Groddeck, Abraham, Eitingon, Reich. . . .

Freud and Ferenczi visited one another. Ferenczi gave hospitality to Anna Freud in Hungary, supplied the Freud family with food and patients during and after the war; Freud kept Ferenczi informed about happenings in his family, and the fate of his sons in the war. They wrote about cigars, flour, missing the morning shower, the political situation, mutual friends and acquaintances, about Ferenczi's military service, the lack of fuel in post-war winters, financial problems, and Freud's grandchildren. Months before their journeys they began to study Baedeker and train and boat timetables.

There was also controversy, conflict, taking offence, and misunderstandings. In 1910, during holidays together in Palermo, Ferenczi refused to allow Freud to dictate him notes on the Schreber case, and for the rest of the journey neither was able to speak about this incident and its emotional importance. Freud criticized, both openly and covertly, Ferenczi's behaviour towards Gizella and Elma Pálos. He was annoyed that Ferenczi had "involved himself so deeply" with Rank (F/Fer, 12.10.1924). He feared that his "Paladin and secret Grand Vizier" wanted to take a "step towards creating a new and oppositional analysis" (F/Fer, 13.12.1929), and imagined Ferenczi going forwards "in all sorts of directions", which seemed to him "to lead to no worthwhile goal". He could only conceive of Ferenczi's "maturing" after finding "a way to turn back" (F/Fer, 13.12.1929). Freud criticized with biting irony Ferenczi's "technique of maternal tenderness" (F/Fer, 13.12.1931) and saw the latter's creative regression as a game with "dream children" on a "fantasy island" from which only violent means could tear him away (F/Fer, 12.5.1932). Lastly, he expressed himself with considerable bitterness: "In the next sentence you accuse yourself, and with this I can only agree [Ferenczi had written: "more courage and more open speech on my side . . . would have been better" (Fer/F, 27.9.32).] For two years you have deliberately turned away from me, and have apparently developed a personal enmity, which goes farther than could be expressed" (Fer/F, 2.10.1932).

Ferenczi criticized Freud's failure to "see through and to bring out the transference of negative feelings and fantasies" in his analysis and his neglect of the healing process (F/Fer, 17.1.1930). Ferenczi resisted a diagnosis of his immersion in therapeutic problems as a "symptom" (Fer/F, 19.5.1932) and wrote of "the depth of my shock" (Fer/F, 27.9.1932) after their last meeting, when they had disagreed about whether Ferenczi should—or might be allowed to—give his planned lecture on "Confusion of Tongues between Adults and the Child" (Ferenczi, 1933 [294]) at the approaching conference in Wiesbaden, and at the end of which Freud did not even shake his hand in farewell.

Shortly afterwards Ferenczi, who was already showing signs of his fatal illness, made a note "about shock" . . . "perhaps even the organs which secure self-preservation, give up their function or reduce it to a minimum. . . ." (1938 [308], 1920–32, p. 253). Ferenczi expressed his criticism of Freud even more in his *Clinical Diary* than in his letters (Ferenczi, 1985 [1932]; cf. also foreword by J. Dupont). However, we also know that when Freud was shown Ferenczi's unpublished work after the latter's death, he expressed "his admiration . . . for the ideas which had hitherto been unknown to him" (Balint, in Ferenczi, 1985 [1932]).

Would it not be presumptuous to reduce this relationship to pure "transference" or to assign to one or other of the protagonists all the "blame" for their dialogue going off the rails?

The controversy did not end with desertion and enmity, but nevertheless it could not be cleared up again. "The disagreements between us . . . can wait . . . it is more important to me that you regain your health", wrote Freud on 2 April 1933. A few weeks later Ferenczi died.

II

The relationship between Freud and Ferenczi was one of friendship and of controversy—and psychoanalysis was always interwoven: psychoanalysis as theory, technique, and movement, but also as personal experience.

On their journey to America, Freud, Ferenczi, and Jung analysed one another. We know what a deep impression it made on Jung when Freud, at a certain point, refused to be analysed any further (Jung, 1962). We know about the relationship between Jung, Sabina Spielrein, and Freud (Carotenuto, 1981). Freud had given many of his disciples a short analysis—often, for example, while out walking (as with Eitingon) (Jones, 1955, p. 31). He even analysed his own daughter Anna—"Annerl's analysis will be fine, other cases are not interesting"—in a letter dated 20 October 1918. On the other hand, Freud refused to analyse certain people, such as Tausk (Roazen, 1969), Federn (Roazen, 1971, p. 310), Reich (p. 493), or Otto Gross, against whose treatment "my egoism, or perhaps rather my self protection, had rebelled" (F/Ju, 19.5.1908). Both Groddeck (1974, p. 88) and Ferenczi (Fer/F, 26.2.1926; 1.3.1926) offered to take him into analysis, but Freud refused. Ferenczi and Groddeck analysed one another, Ferenczi analysed Jones, Freud his lady friend Loé Kann, and they corresponded about this. Ferenczi thought that Freud should analyse Jung (Fer/F, 20.1.1912) and vehemently contradicted Otto Rank, who, during the controversy about him and his *Trauma of Birth* (1924), had expressed the opinion that it was an advantage for him not to have been analysed himself (Fer/F, 1.9.1924).

On 14 July 1911 Ferenczi wrote to Freud that he had taken Elma, the daughter of his lady friend Gizella (Pálos by marriage), into analysis. Gizella, too, had already been analysed by him. In the course of her analysis Ferenczi fell in love with Elma Pálos, who entered "victorious into his heart" (Fer/F, 3.12.1911). He begged

Freud to take over the analysis, and despite his doubts Freud agreed. Later he kept Ferenczi informed about the details of this treatment, and in particular whether and how Elma's love for Ferenczi will "stand up to" the analysis. All of those concerned committed indiscretions: Ferenczi sent Freud copies of Elma's letters, in which she "wants to know what you (Freud) have written to me about her . . ." (Fer/F, 18.1.1912). Freud wrote confidentially about Ferenczi to Frau Gizella (17.12.1911)—and, of course, Gizella showed the letter to Ferenczi. In addition, Elma's father, to whom she had communicated details of the analysis, wanted to intervene. Ferenczi visited Freud in Vienna to talk to him about Elma. This meeting was kept secret from Elma, who lived in Vienna. Although Elma wished to continue her analysis, Freud broke it off when, by his reckoning, she had reached "the narcissistic current" (F/Fer, 13.3.1912). Back in Budapest, Elma returned to analysis with Ferenczi. By this means he hoped to achieve certainty about her feelings. He resisted her "arts of war (tenderness)" (Fer/F, 27.5.1912) and remained abstinent in a "rather cruel way" (Fer/F, 18.7.1912) but still did not achieve clarity about his own or Elma's feelings. On the other hand "poor Elma has no enjoyment at all . . . (from the analysis)" (Fer/F, 26.7.1912). In the end Ferenczi abandoned Elma's analysis. (In "Psychoanalysis and Telepathy" (1941d [1921], pp. 191–192) Freud reports a similar triangle in which a daughter was submitted to analysis because the man concerned could not decide between her and her mother.)

Elma married an American called Laurvik, but this marriage did not last long. Years later, in 1919, Frau Gizella and Sándor Ferenczi married. On the way to the registry office they heard that Géza Pálos, Gizella's divorced husband, had died. Ferenczi suffered for years from the effects of this event; he complained of depression and hypochondriacal symptoms and had great difficulty in regaining his balance. It was characteristic for his temperament that he should throw himself unreservedly and without any "insurance" into the therapeutic situation, and that he should do so little to draw a clear and protective line between his professional and his private life. Not only the analyst but the whole man Ferenczi was involved in this relationship, and he went to the outer limits with a degree of courage that was his strength and also—in this episode—his weakness.

We see Freud pulled to and fro between deep sympathy for Ferenczi's and Gizella Pálos's fate—a sympathy that drove him to intervene—and doubts about the effect of such an intervention. He "worried about linking the fate of our friendship to something different and unpredictable" (F/Fer, 21.4.1912), and he wrote of "the danger of personal estrangement caused by analysis" (4.5.1913). He saw the danger more clearly than did Ferenczi, and nevertheless he analysed Elma and later Ferenczi too. On one occasion he described himself as an "emotional donkey whom . . . even gray hair does not prevent from making a fool of himself" (F/Fer, 23.1.1912) and on another as "hard-hearted"—albeit "from sympathy and softness" (Freud to Frau Gizella, 17.12.1911).

In other relationships with followers and patients Freud varied between an "emotional" and a "hard-hearted" approach, between a type of relationship that he called "unpronounced" transference (1914g, p. 151), where he allowed considerable closeness—"because I like it . . ." (F/Fer, 6.10.1910)—gave presents, and invited them to meals (Haynal, 1987, p. 7), a fact that he scarcely analysed or not at all, and another type of relationship, in which he "tended towards intolerance" towards "neurotics" (F/Fer, 20.1.1930), and in which he could keep his distance, "frustrate their tricks" (F/Fer, 20.7.1912), and show considerable "cooling off" in the face of their transference wishes (F/Fer, 24.3.1912). His was a difficult position: many were disappointed not to find in him that "psychoanalytic superman" (F/Fer, 6.10.1910) that they had "constructed" (F/Fer, 6.10.1910), and whatever he did, there were critics.

For Freud the unverbalized area had a great deal to do with a saying of Vischer's that he liked to quote: "As to morals, that goes without saying" (Freud, 1905a, p. 267). He could not and would not take up an analytic stance towards people for whom morals were not self-evident, but he passed judgement on them—and who shall deny him the right—in accordance with the morality that was self-evident to him as man, doctor, professor, father of a family, and founder and leader of a new movement in the Vienna of his time. Thus he said, for example, that Stekel "offended against every aspect of good taste" (F/Ju, 24.7.1911) and that there were things that a "gentleman" should not do, even unconsciously (Freud about Jung, when the latter gave Jones an incorrect date for a meeting—two slightly different versions in Jones, 1959, p. 221, and Jones, 1955, p. 145).

Freud's followers and patients found themselves in a dilemma when, on the one hand, he did not allow certain aspects of his role to be discussed and, on the other, indicated that his opposite number should "tear himself out of his infantile role" (F/Fer, 2.10.1910).

This was Elma's dilemma and also Ferenczi's. The latter could not accept a relationship being divided into a verbalized and an unverbalized—because self-evident—part. Everything can and should be verbalized between analytically trained people. "Only think what that would mean, if one could speak the truth to everyone: to one's father, one's teacher, one's neighbour and even the king" (Fer/F, 5.2.1910). And analysis seemed to Ferenczi to be the means by which even the hidden and unutterable could be brought to light and put into words.

Puzzled and uncertain in the face of the complications produced by his involvement, Sándor Ferenczi resorted over and over again to analysis as a tool. He started with the hope of having in analysis an objective method of clarifying human relationships. Thus he thought that every fully analysed analyst must "inevitably come to the same conclusions . . . and will consequently adopt the same tactical and technical method" for any specified patient (Ferenczi, 1928 [283], p. 89). He compared the process with chemical reactions "in a test-tube" (Fer/F, 21.4.1909). Neither in Elma's analysis, however, nor in Ferenczi's with Freud could psychoanalysis produce that measure of chemically pure emotion, untouched by transference or neurosis. On the contrary: the relationship became not simpler, but more difficult.

Precisely during this episode Ferenczi had painfully to realize, both as analyst and as analysand, that psychoanalysis is not a tool that can function independently of the person using it. Very probably these events played a major part in making Ferenczi recognize the analyst's attitude as a variable in the therapeutic equation and therefore placing this at the centre of his interest. In the same way as he suffered from not being able to distinguish between "transference" and "real" feelings in this web of relationships, and from the divisions between the roles of analyst, analysand, lover, friend, and disciple, and in the same way as he involved himself with his whole personality in this relationship, so, also, was he able to see with extreme clarity how patients suffered under the "hypocrisy" (Ferenczi, 1933 [294], pp. 158–159) of phenomena of intended "abstinence" on the part of the analyst.

A consistent line can be followed from these experiences to his technical experiments, to active therapy and relaxation methods, and, further, to mutual analysis and to his theoretical concept of the "Confusion of Tongues between Adults and the Child" (Ferenczi, 1933 [294]), the role of adults, and the psychological atmosphere during development and as a result of trauma.

III

It is tempting to pass judgement, from a supposedly superior position, on Ferenczi's and Freud's entanglement, their use and misuse of psychoanalysis, their indiscretions and acting out. As if present-day analysts, with all their training, their personal analysis and supervision, and with all the theoretical and technical equipment that have since been provided, found it any easier to achieve optimal separation between their *professional* and *private* lives. How many analysts marry their patients, how many finish by sleeping with them (Chertok, 1983; Fischer, 1977), how much is there between parent-and-child generations of analysts that can never be verbalized and worked through.

Analysis is, in Freud's words: "actually a *healing through love*" (F/Ju, 6.12.1906, emphasis added). (Note that a similar idea—"our cures are cures of love"—is to be found a few months later in the Minutes of the Wednesday Society, where Freud says that the "power" in the treatment lies in the transference love and that the patient is "compelled" to give up his resistances by his love for us (Nunberg & Federn, 1962, meeting of 1 October 1907, p. 101). For Freud, the term "love" probably means "transference love", and for Ferenczi also "countertransference love" (Leopold Szondi, a psychotherapist in the Ferenczi tradition, often refers to the therapist as a "soul donor"—by analogy with the term "blood donor"). In this connection Eitingon quotes Freud as pronouncing the same sentence and adding that, by dint of enormous personal effort, it might be possible to overcome even more difficulties in the treatment, but that one would "lose his skin by doing so" (Ruitenbeek, 1973, p. 445). In choosing this quotation from Freud for the title of this chapter, I intended a play on this double meaning. For this reason, the attempt to work with transfer pictures of emotions is bound to fail—"when all is said and done, it is impossible to destroy anyone *in absentia* or *in effigie*" (Freud, 1912b, p. 108). Otherwise one is behaving "like the less than potent man who said to his young wife after the first coitus on their wedding night: now you know what it is like: all the rest is just repetition" (F/Fer, 20.1.1930).

Why do we tend to think that "technique then was not so developed as it is today"—as if today we had access to a definite and undoubted technique, and only the first generation of analysts were in a phase of "experimentation"—to adopt Ferenczi's expression? In fact, one might just as well say that analysts then were aware that it is always a matter of experimentation, and that from the moment when we spoke of classical technique, we entered a phase of illusions: the illusion that there could be a technique that one only needed to learn and apply "correctly" and about which even textbooks could be written.

* * *

We have reached the year 1932—one year before Ferenczi's sixtieth birthday. He was 35 when he came to know Freud; a bare quarter-century of intense friendship lay in-between, decades of the painful and satisfying work of an analyst, who wanted to go as far as possible with the means at his disposal, who tried passionately to understand himself and his analysands (a term introduced and first used by Ferenczi—1915 [181 in 309], p. 81), with a passion that many—including Freud—considered exaggerated, because in his desire to help it drove him to the very bounds of possibility.

Ferenczi was no longer willing to judge himself in the mirror of his master's approval or disapproval, and he decided to take his inquiries as far as possible in the form of a clinical diary. This *Clinical Diary*, covering nine months (from 7 January to 2 October 1932), is certainly a step towards self-assertion and an attempt to understand all the depths of an analyst's position, without recourse to the dialogue and interaction of correspondence; nevertheless the transference figure of Freud, the imagined addressee of this *Diary*, can be clearly discerned.

As it happens, we know from Michael Balint (1969i, p. 14) that Freud, as stated, did indeed—albeit after Ferenczi's death—look into certain of his fragments and notes; moreover, that he did so with great interest and respect.

When an analyst considers the whole of his life and work up to a certain point with such depth of self-inquiry, this cannot be defined by the alternatives of orthodoxy or heterodoxy—however such terms are defined. The problem is stated on the first page: "the analyst's *lack of feeling*". We are in the midst of the subject: the analyst's "real countertransference", the need to know more about it, and the idea—almost like a caricature—of "mutual" analysis. Ferenczi himself describes the connection: "Mutual analysis will also be less terribly demanding, will promote more genial and helpful approach in the patient, instead of the unremittingly all-too-good, selfless demeanor, behind which exhaustion, unpleasure, even murderous intentions are hidden" (1985 [1932], p. 16).

In the following passage Ferenczi relates this atmosphere to his ideas about the *body* and *trauma*: "The final result of analysis of the transference may be the establishment of a benevolent, passionless atmosphere, such as may have existed before the trauma" (p. 27).

In mutual analysis one finds "that common ground . . . (that) is present in every case of infantile trauma. And is finding this . . . the necessary condition for understanding and for the flowing over of healing sympathy?" (p. 15).

Ferenczi's concept of trauma complements Freud's. Whereas Freud concentrated on discovering intra-psychic happenings, Ferenczi centred on the individual's relationship to the reality around him and investigated the different ways in which the organism responds to the changing environment—be it in phylogenetic speculation in his "Thalassa: A Theory of Genitality" (1924 [268]), be it in his questions about the relationship between adult and child, analyst and analysand.

Ferenczi approached the traumatic event and its working through in therapy from a social point of view ("Psychoanalysis is . . . a social phenomenon", he wrote to Groddeck—Fer/Grod, 11.10.1922). Before trauma there was an atmosphere of trust between the individual (the child) and his social surroundings (the adults) (first phase), which is destroyed by an extreme rise in tension in the relationship (second phase). The child seeks help from precisely that person or those persons who were responsible for this rise in the emotional temperature of the relationship in the first place. If this help is not forthcoming (third phase), there will be a split within the personality, giving rise to one part that suffers under this intolerable situation and another that observes unemotionally and as from a distance and offers comfort, in fact tries to take over the assistant ego functions that should have been carried out by the outer world. The result is a permanently disturbed relationship to social reality: the Self, the "outer layer" (Freud, 1940a [1938], p. 145) of the psychic organization, has withdrawn so far "within" that it can no longer discharge its function of interchange.

In therapy Ferenczi tried to revive the traumatic sequence in order to find a new resolution by offering what had previously not been offered: a trustful atmosphere—in Balint's words: "an innocent, unconditional one" (Balint, 1933e, p. 165). This, he hoped, would enable the analysand to heal the split in his personality. On the analyst's part this requires a particular kind of listening and sensibility, in order to find the causes of the suffering. The analysand must feel a real sympathy, and for Ferenczi it is this atmosphere that makes it possible to project the trauma into the past and to communicate it as a memory. In contrast to the traumatizing situation, the analysand feels confident. It is not free association alone that brings "true healing", but the doctor's engagement; if he is not fully engaged, he must admit this honestly—in contrast to the way adults behave with children.

The countertransference becomes an important tool and the analyst's weaknesses and errors "fortunate sins" (Augustine). According to Ferenczi, one can almost say that the more an analyst shows weaknesses that lead him into making larger or smaller mistakes that can then be discovered and rectified, the better the chance of the analysis developing a sincere and authentic relationship.

Thus the analyst's "strength" is defined through his way of dealing with his "weakness". The light thrown on this countertransference has advantages for the analyst as well. In one case this communication of Ferenczi's mental state developed into a form of mutual analysis from which, he tells us, he, the analyst, derived considerable benefit.

However, Ferenczi quickly recognized the "dilemma" of mutual analysis (Ferenczi, 1985, p. 28) and the dangers and limitations that restrict its use: mutual analysis can only be carried out in relation to the needs of the analysand and the ability of the analyst to proceed with it in a given clinical situation. In any case, mutual analysis can, according to Ferenczi, only be an emergency measure.

Ferenczi sees the end of an analysis like another life situation: at the end of schooling, school-friends part without tragic scenes, knowing that school friendships are not meant for life—each must go on to develop further according to his own life's plan. Ferenczi would also imagine the end of a happy parent–child relationship in a similar way.

Ferenczi's methods led him to regard Freud's attitude—despite the latter's recognition of emotion in the transference—as intellectualized and impersonal. He came to place great stress on the importance of the analyst's own analysis. An analysis without any obligation would be ideal. For him, the best analyst is a cured patient. The student must first recognize his illness in order to recover. Ferenczi questions the value of supervised analysis, noting that in a sense the patient is controlling the analyst in any case. The analyst should refrain from unconsciously using analysands instead of letting them develop.

Looking back, Ferenczi describes the way he has come. Freud had told him that patients were "riffraff" and psychoanalysis of no value as therapy:

> This was the point at which I refused to follow him. Against his will I began to deal openly with questions of technique. I refused to abuse the patients' trust in this way, and neither did I share his idea that therapy was worthless. I believed rather, that therapy was good, but perhaps we were still deficient, and I began to look for our errors. (Ferenczi, 1985 [1932], p. 186)

Ferenczi describes his "errors"—namely, following Rank "too far", because he was dazzled by his insight on the transference situation. He thought later that he also went too far in his relaxation technique and considered that after these mistakes he could work "humanely and naturally, with benevolence, and free from personal prejudices, on the acquisition of knowledge that will allow me to help" (1985 [1932], p. 186).

This was his programme. The concepts he derived from his method are remarkable. His notes on the sacrifice of "women's interests" reads like a radical feminist critique:

> One example: the castration theory of femininity. Fr[eud] believes that the clitoris develops and functions earlier than the vagina, that is, girls are born with the feeling that they have a penis, and only later do they learn to renounce both this and the mother and to accept vaginal and uterine femininity. Thus he neglects the alternative possibility, that instinctual heterosexual orientation (perhaps only in fantasy) is highly developed quite early on and that masculinity only takes its place for traumatic reasons (primal scene) as a hysterical symptom.
>
> The author may have a personal aversion to spontaneous female-oriented sexuality in women: idealization of the mother. He recoils from the task of having a sexually demanding mother, and having to satisfy her. At some point his mother's passionate nature may have presented him with such a task. (The primal scene may have rendered him relatively impotent.)
>
> The *castration of the father, the potent one, as a reaction to the humiliation he experienced, led to the construction of a theory in which the father castrates the son* and, moreover, is then revealed by the son as a god. In his conduct Fr[eud] plays only the role of this castrating god, he wants to ignore the traumatic moment of his own castration in childhood; he is the only one who does not have to be analysed. (Ferenczi, 1985 [1932], p. 188, underlined in the original)

Hard, for many perhaps shocking, words, but perhaps also rousing ones, in line with his passionate appeal to take up a personal inner psychoanalytic attitude and behaviour again, instead of a projective position, holding that what is stated as truth or unassailable dogma can secure the future of psychoanalysis or our own. Psychoanalysis must constantly and repeatedly ask questions—or cease to exist as such.

It seems important, with regard to clarifying our own past and traditions as analysts, to recognize that the analyst's involvement in the analysis, his countertransference in the wider sense of the word, his employment of his own sensibility, the broader use of psychoanalysis for suffering people, whatever their diagnosis—all this had been investigated, and in some sense practised to the limits of possibility, by one of the great pioneers of psychoanalysis.

Various factors have led to this pioneer's work and to the discussion, the dialogue, between these two pioneers—a historical fact of the greatest importance for the psychoanalytic movement—falling into oblivion. These factors may in part be related to Freud, his limitations and his age, but probably owe more to the relationships among analysts and their fears of and resistance to re-questioning, or even giving up, positions that they had thought were sure and safe. They have been recalled from this complete repression only thanks to the efforts of the British "Middle Group", under the influence of Michael Balint, Ferenczi's literary executor, and the independent spirit of people like Donald W. Winnicott and Paula Heimann. It seems to us essential to the self-image of analysts that our recognized history should once again be based on the actual facts that gave this story its form. This could help analysis, free it from a certain sectarianism and from too great an unanalysed influence of some sorcerers encountered during training. This would restore a historical perspective to the century of remarkable adventure investigating the inner life—that adventure, which is typical for the psychoanalytic movement, which itself was started by a genius and continued by outstanding people, one of whom was distinguished, not only by great charm and generosity, but also by intellectual courage and uncommon honesty—Sándor Ferenczi.

CHAPTER THREE

Problems of psychoanalytic practice in the 1920s

In our view, the story begins in 1918, at the Fifth International Psychoanalytic Congress in Budapest, the culmination point in Sándor Ferenczi's professional life—a few years after Freud had written about him that, until then, "Hungary . . . has produced only one collaborator, S. Ferenczi, but one that indeed outweighs a whole society" (Freud, 1914d, p. 33). In fact, in the 1910s and 1920s Ferenczi was the only one, apart from Otto Rank, Freud's closest friend and collaborator. Looking back, Freud said in 1933 that their relationship had been even more than mere friendship—namely, an "intimate sharing of life, feelings and interests" (F/Fer, 11.1.1933). At this Budapest Congress, in September 1918, Freud's lecture, "Lines of Advance in Psycho-Analytic Therapy" (1919a [1918]), was to be his swan-song on the subject of psychoanalytic technique; in it he spoke about "a new field of analytic technique"—which, however, "is still in the course of being evolved" (p. 162).

Indeed, Freud would never again take up this question in public: he seemed to prefer to leave it to his intellectual circle, offering encouragement in the form, among others, of a prize for the best study on the correlation of theory and technique (Freud, 1922d).

Apparently, his hopes were high. Ferenczi and Rank, in particular, would take up the challenge and write seminal works on the issue.

The technique at issue

Ferenczi and Rank had originally intended to submit a jointly written book, *The Development of Psychoanalysis* (Ferenczi & Rank, 1924), for the abovementioned prize. In the end, however, they had given up the idea, feeling that neither their work, nor any other in the field, could do justice to the overall problem (cf. their Preface in Ferenczi & Rank, 1924). In their book they concluded that, instead of remembering (cf. Freud, 1914g), the *repetition* of infantile material should play "*the chief rôle in analytic technique*" (p. 4; emphasis in original), although the repeated material should then gradually be transformed into actual remembering (p. 4). Furthermore, this material should be consistently interpreted in its relation to the "analytic situation". As to technique, they introduce the method of setting "a definite period of time for completing the last part of the treatment" (p. 13). In advocating the reliving of past scenes in the present analytic situation, they stressed again, as Freud did in his early writings, the importance of *emotions* [*Gefühle*]—although in a different and more developed form, under the keyword "experience" [*Erlebnis*].

At first, Freud—who had been informed about the work in progress, had read the proofs, and had given "valuable advice" (Fer/F, 30.1.1924)—accepted in essence Ferenczi's and Rank's point of view. In a circular letter to the Secret Committee he stated: "I value the joint book as a correction of my view of the role of repetition or acting out in analysis" (F/Abr, 15.2.1924). He saw it as "a refreshing intervention that may possibly precipitate changes in our present analytic habits" (F/Abr, 15.2.1924, p. 346). Having acknowledged the new contribution, he added, however, that "personally, I shall continue with 'classical' analysis" (F/Abr, 15.2.1924).

Still more than *The Development of Psychoanalysis*, Otto Rank's book on *The Trauma of Birth*, published in the same year (1924), was to become a stumbling-block and was, furthermore, to symbolize the later alienation between Rank and the other members of the Committee. For Rank, the psychophysical trauma of birth, experienced by the infant as a separation from the mother, was the foundation and the core of the unconscious; psychoanalytic therapy consisted in subsequently bringing to a close the incompletely mastered birth trauma. The transference libido, which has to be analytically dissolved for both sexes, was in his view the maternal transference libido, as it existed in the prenatal physiological bond between mother and child. Birth anxiety was seen as the root of any anxiety, intra-uterine pleasure as the origin of any later pleasure. In fact, Rank's interest in the "maternal libido" dates back at least to 1907. Discussing Freud's presentation of the "Rat Man" case in the Wednesday Society, Rank remarked that "all factors clearly point to the patient's love for his mother, even though there has not yet been any direct reference to this in the analytic material" (Nunberg & Federn, 1962, p. 233).

How did the other members of Freud's inner circle react to these new concepts? There had been considerable personal tension within the group for a couple of years. From about 1922 onward, Otto Rank and Ernest Jones had been quarrelling over competencies in psychoanalytic publishing. Rank, director of the *Verlag* in Vienna, claimed an overall responsibility for any publication; on the other hand Jones, head of the *Press* in London, wanted to control all English publications. Apart from financial problems, this posed the question of the locus of power and of the extent to which the English *Press* was or was not to be allowed to steer an independent course. Freud, for his part, took a clear position: he supported Rank and criticized Jones for his "unjust susceptibilities" and for having "less control of [his] moods and passions, [being] less consistent, sincere, and reliable than [Freud] had a right to expect" of him (F/Jo, 7.1.1922; Jones, 1957, p. 53). Although Jones tried to present his point of view (Jo/F, 10.4.1922; Brome, 1982, p. 143), this did nothing to change Freud's: he considered Jones's behaviour—as he wrote to Rank (F/R, 8.7.1922)[1]—"in fact meant

---

[1] The letters between Freud and Rank, partly published by Taft (1958) and Lieberman (1985), were kindly made available to us by Judith Dupont, Hélène Rank Veltfort, and John Balint. The Rank/Ferenczi correspondence, quoted later on, is also part of this Freud/Rank convolute.

for me but directed towards you". Freud did not hesitate to side with Rank: "*We* can understand Jones's reaction" (F/R, 20.7.1922; emphasis added). Freud even told Rank that he would prefer him to any other person as leader of the psychoanalytic movement (F/R, 4.6.1922). In addition to Freud, Rank was also supported by Ferenczi. Freud, who had initiated a closer relationship between them, appreciated this "intimacy", this "harmony", this "alliance"—as he wrote both to Ferenczi and to Rank (F/Fer, 24.8.1922; F/R, 24.8.1922, 8.9.1922). In the autumn of 1912 Freud had invited Rank and Ferenczi to spend a couple of days with him in London. In Freud's view the journey should "also have the goal to bring about a more intimate relationship between you [Rank] and Ferenczi" (F/R, 25.8.1912). In the end, because Freud's daughter Mathilde had had an abortion, Freud did not want to leave her, and the visit did not take place. At the same time, cooperation and even friendship was slowly growing between Jones and Karl Abraham in Berlin, as evidenced by the Abraham/Jones correspondence (Karl Abraham Archives, Library of Congress). Our material does not allow us to assess the role of Hanns Sachs clearly. Sachs, a friend of Rank's, was in close contact with Freud *and* with Abraham, as was Max Eitingon, who might also have been informed by Anna Freud (Young-Bruehl, 1988, *passim*). We know, however, that Eitingon, at least, was only gradually "let into" the secret by Freud himself, as the latter wrote to Rank (F/R, 8.9.1922).

The situation within the Committee was coming to a head, and Rank was already speaking of its dissolution. In accordance with Ferenczi and Rank, Freud intervened with a circular letter to the members of the Committee (26.11.1922)[2]; in this, he not only stood up for Rank, but he interpreted Jones's and Abraham's behaviour as being governed by ambivalent feelings toward himself, directing their hostile aspect towards Rank. Freud drew two conclusions: (1) he declared that he would not participate in the next meeting of the Committee; and (2) he proposed that "Jones should complete the short analysis he had with Ferenczi" (26.11.1922). In fact, Jones

---

[2] Rank Archives, Columbia University, New York. Sets of the Circular Letters (in total numbering more than 400), all of them incomplete, are kept in various archives. A complete set is being compiled by Drs Wittenberger, Junker, and Friedrich, with publication in view.

had been analysed for two months by Ferenczi in Budapest in the summer of 1913. . . .

In August 1923, in San Cristoforo in South Tyrol, the meeting of the Committee was marked by a heated controversy between Rank and Jones. As he had predicted, Freud—who spent his holidays nearby—did not participate. He had felt ill for some time, and his doctor, Felix Deutsch, had already diagnosed his cancer—a diagnosis that Deutsch had not disclosed to Freud, but he had told Otto Rank. This information might have contributed to Rank's state of mind, but it cannot wholly explain, as Jones supposed (1957, pp. 57–58), the dispute between the two of them. It was, more probably, an anti-Semitic remark about Rank made by Jones to Abraham A. Brill some time before the meeting that infuriated Rank. From Jones's letter to his wife (26.8.1922) we know that: "We have spent the whole day thrashing out the Rank–Jones affair. Very painful but I hope our relations will now be better and believe so, but on the other hand expect Ferenczi will hardly speak to me for Brill has just been there and told him I had said Rank was a swindling Jew (stark übertrieben)" [German in original] (Brome, 1982, p. 139). Rank at once brought up the matter and demanded Jones's expulsion from the Committee. Abraham defended Jones, who had no choice but keep silent. Jones himself confessed later in a letter to Karl Abraham (12 Nov. 1924) that he "had not the courage to defend" his "famous remark at San Cristoforo".

In general, the scientific discussion duplicated the personal conflicts, and two lines of thought became more distinct, with Ernest Jones and the Berlin school (Karl Abraham, Max Eitingon, Hanns Sachs) at one pole and Rank and the Budapest group at the other. Max Eitingon—considered as a possible compromise candidate for the presidency of the International Psycho-Analytical Association (IPA) instead of Ernest Jones—was the one to break the news to Freud that the two books had exploded "like a bomb" in the Committee (Eit/F, 31.1.1924)[3]. Eitingon, for his part, although praising

---

[3]Copies of the voluminous Freud/Eitingon correspondence, the publication of which is being prepared by M. Schröter, are kept in the archives of the Freud Museum, London, and in the archives of S. Freud Copyrights, Wivenhoe. We thank Erica Davies, Michael Molnar, Mark Paterson, and Thomas Roberts for giving us access to them. The translations from the original German are ours.

the new concept of the "analytic situation" in the joint book as having "great merit", dismissed Rank's claim to have found "a very short lever arm, indeed a mere knack, to move a mighty weight and to unhinge the world of illness" as "extremely unlikely" (Eit/F, 31.1.1924). Hanns Sachs, who had always been in close contact and on friendly terms with Rank, with whom he edited the journal *Imago* and had cooperated on a book (Rank & Sachs, 1913), felt particularly hurt that Rank had not disclosed anything about his new ideas to him. He wrote to Freud (according to Rank's letter to Ferenczi, 20.3.1924) that if Rank and Ferenczi really intended to replace the former theory with their new one, he would find this as irreconcilable with psychoanalysis as the directions taken by Jung or Adler. Theoretically, he put his finger on a tender spot in Rank's work: its missing clinical basis, reducing the whole exposition to "an analogy" and the book to "a torso" (Sa/F, 20.2.1924; in Jones, 1957, p. 66). Ernest Jones voiced similar objections, but the most severe criticism was raised by Abraham: "Results of whatever kind obtained in a *legitimate analytic manner* would never give me cause for such grave doubts. This is something different. I see signs of an ominous development concerning vital issues of psycho-analysis" (Abr/F, 21.2.1924). Both books would be "manifestations of a regression in the scientific field, the symptoms of which agree in every small detail with those of Jung's secession from psychoanalysis." They represented a "turning away from . . . psycho-analytic method" (Abr/F, 26.2.1924). "My criticisms are not directed at the results achieved by Ferenczi and Rank but against the methods they used. These seem to me to lead away from psycho-analysis" (Abr/F, 8.3.1924).

Although Rank did not inform Abraham, Eitingon, Jones, or Sachs of his ideas in any detail before their publication, Ferenczi and Freud, at least, knew of them (here Jones [1957, p. 60] is mistaken). Freud may even have received a copy of the manuscript as a birthday present in May 1923; in fact, Rank's book was published with the following dedication: "Presented to Sig. Freud, explorer of the unconscious, creator of psychoanalysis, May 6, 1923" ["Sig. Freud, dem Erforscher des Unbewußten, Schöpfer der Psychoanalyse, überreicht zum 6. Mai 1923"]. Freud accepted the dedication explicitly (F/R, 1.12.1923) and was positively impressed by Rank's "discovery", which he found "really great" (F/Fer,

1.6.1923). But Freud's appreciation was not without ambivalence; in associating to one of his dreams, he confessed to Rank that he identified himself with "the boasting giant Goliath" and Rank with the "feared David, who will carry through the devaluation of my work with his trauma of birth" (F/R, 26.11.1923). But only five days later he wrote to Rank: "I myself am paralysed now, I am extremely happy about your being so beautifully productive. Doesn't it also mean for me: Non omnis moriar [I will not die completely (Horace, *Odes*)]. Your Freud" Paralysed and happy . . . was the giant Goliath to survive in young David or to be destroyed by him?

Freud summarized his point of view in the above-quoted circular letter of 15 February 1924. He appreciated Rank's work as "a very important book, that . . . has given me a great deal to think about"—although he had "not yet formed [his] final opinion about it" (Freud & Abraham, 1965a, p. 346). In the following weeks and months, however, Freud became more and more critical—but still in a cautious and careful way. Although his first reaction had been to say: "I do not know if [of Rank's book] 33 or 66% are true, but in any case this is the most important progress since the discovery of psychoanalysis" (F/Fer, 24.3.1924), he was more and more "on the way from the 66% to the 33%" (F/Fer, 26.3.1924). He confessed to Rank (as he wrote to Ferenczi; F/Fer, 20.3.1924): "My esteem for . . . [the] trauma of birth is rather regressing than progressing."

At the same time, Freud asked Ferenczi and Rank not to take his criticisms personally: "My trust in you and Rank is unconditional" (F/Fer, 20.3.1924). Rank nevertheless felt deeply disappointed. In various discussions and long letters (cf., e.g., R/Fer, 20.3.1924; R/F, 24.3.1924) he tried to convince Freud anew. Although these discussions were "on completely friendly terms" (R/Fer, 20.3.1924), it became more and more clear that Freud would not be persuaded; he even began to write an article criticizing Rank's theory, which was published as "The dissolution of the Oedipus complex" (Freud 1924d). Freud did not, however, include the passages that dealt with Rank's concept. Rank, all the more disappointed, developed a "stubborn" attitude, which added to his alienation from his former friends. He leant more and more on Ferenczi who—for the moment—remained his only confidant.

Ferenczi's position was becoming particularly difficult. On the one hand, he was fascinated by Rank's theory and found his modifications of psychoanalytic technique useful for his own practice (Fer/F, 24.3.1924); on the other, he was anxious not to disagree with Freud, and he found it unimaginable that he might be considered a heretic. What Ferenczi tried to do in this uncomfortable sandwich position is to calm Rank and to convince Freud of the merits of Rank's theory. Evidently, Ferenczi's strategy did not work out, and he would have to make his own decision.

Personal conflicts threatened to overshadow the scientific importance of this discussion. Freud, in trying to lead its participants back to science, pointed to the different aims of the "old" and the "new" techniques (F/Committee, 15.2.1924; Freud & Abraham, 1965a, pp. 344–348)—one aiming at insight, the other at experiencing—and advocated a calm application of *both* techniques and an investigation of their respective theoretical results. In his opinion, the differences would not necessitate a personal and scientific split: "We could remain under the same roof with the greatest equanimity, and after a few years' work it would become plain whether one side had exaggerated a useful [sic] finding or the other had underrated it" (F/Abr, 4.3.1924). In fact, it was *technique* that was at the centre of the discussion. A modification of technique by Freud (Freud, 1918b [1914])—the fact of fixing a time limit for the termination of the cure—had been at the origin of Rank's ideas concerning birth trauma: "The mere fact of always fixing a limit gave Rank the opportunity to discover the repetition, during analysis, of the reactions of his patients to the fact of fixing a limit" (Fer/F, 14.2.1924). This also demonstrates (if proof were necessary) the *interdependence of technique and theory*, and even of the theoretical reconstructions that are possible. Although at first Freud was of the opinion that "activity of such a kind on the part of the analysing physician is unobjectionable and entirely justified" (Freud, 1919a [1918], p. 162), he later expressed reservations that might be described as pedagogical: "Ferenczi's 'active therapy' is a dangerous temptation to ambitious beginners" (F/Committee, 15.2.1924; Freud & Abraham, 1965a, p. 346).[4]

---

[4] We have already described the controversial dialogue between Freud and Ferenczi, especially insofar as questions of technique are concerned (chapter two).

Behind this discussion also lies the problem of "insight" [*Einsicht*] in opposition to empathy [*Einfühlung*]. Does the analyst understand the patient's conflicts only with his rational thinking, as the emerging ego-psychology would have it, or is he, as Ferenczi thought very early on, making introjections in identifying himself with aspects of the transference? These questions led Ferenczi, in his *Clinical Diary*, to ask how his own associations about his own history could help him to understand his patient.

Ferenczi's way to the Clinical Diary

Ferenczi did not follow Rank's theoretical and practical concepts. Both being dissatisfied with the results of "classical" analysis, Rank was later to stress the *here-and-now* in the analytic encounter and, finally, in leaving psychoanalysis proper, to develop his "will therapy", whereas Ferenczi would begin to work with ever deeper regressions. Both, however, maintain the crucial role of empathy and experience in opposition to rational insight. Ferenczi continued to experiment with various therapeutic techniques. Having abandoned his "active therapy", which did not achieve lasting results, he tried out what he called "relaxation" or "neo-catharsis". This experiment—which was never a "method" in the strict sense of the word—has often been misunderstood and simply equated with "hugging and kissing". In fact, Ferenczi proceeded from the theoretical concept that the infant or child had been subject to traumata that surpassed his means of coping with them, leading to *"splits in the personality"* [*Spaltung der Persönlichkeit*] (Ferenczi, 1933 [294], p. 165; emphasis added), leading to the picture of *"fragmentation"* or even *"atomization"* (p. 165). As Michael Balint put it: "The central idea, to which Ferenczi returned time and again, is the essential disproportion between the child's limited capacity for dealing with excitation and the adults' unconscious and consequently uncontrolled, passionate and simultaneously guilt-laden, over- or under-stimulating of the child" (Balint, 1949a, pp. 218–219). The therapy should, therefore, provide a trustworthy, "empathic" atmosphere, in which the patient, having relived the traumatic scene(s) under different circumstances, is then able to heal the split.

It is in this context that Ferenczi developed his concept of *trauma*. When he stressed again "the original traumatic factor in our aetiological equations" (Ferenczi, 1930 [291], p. 120) and maintained that "[h]ysterical fantasies do not lie" (p. 121), he spoke *not* primarily of singular traumatic events but of a "confusion of tongues", of a fundamental misunderstanding between two different worlds: the world of the infant and that of the adult. Trauma in this context encompasses the infant's inability to develop a coherent view of himself and the adult world. Writing about sexual traumatization in childhood, Ferenczi stated:

> When the child recovers from such an attack, he feels enormously confused, in fact, split—innocent and culpable at the same time—and his confidence in the testimony of his own senses is broken. Moreover, the harsh behaviour of the adult partner tormented and made angry by his remorse renders the child still more conscious of his own guilt and still more ashamed. Almost always the perpetrator behaves as though nothing had happened. (Ferenczi, 1933 [294], pp. 162–163)

In Ferenczi's view, the truly traumatic event follows the adult's behaviour *after* an intense emotional experience between him/herself and the child (cf. also Ferenczi, 1931 [292], p. 138). "The fear of the uninhibited, almost mad adult changes the child, so to speak, into a psychiatrist" (Ferenczi, 1933 [294], p. 165). In essence, we find here Balint's later concept of the three phases of trauma (Balint, 1969a). In order to enable a healing of the split, the analyst should, according to Ferenczi, avoid what he termed the analyst's "professional hypocrisy"; he should encourage criticism and admit his shortcomings. This will "create in the patient a confidence in the analyst. *It is this confidence that establishes the contrast between the present and the unbearable traumatogenic past*" (Balint, 1969a, p. 160).

This was Ferenczi's position when an exceptional patient of his challenged his empathic and understanding approach: "R.N. [Elisabeth Severn] demands methodically conducted analysis [of the analyst] as the only possible protective measure against the inclination, perceived in me, to kill or torture patients" (Ferenczi, 1985 [1932], p. 11). It was 1932—one year before Ferenczi's sixtieth birthday. He had decided to take his inquiries as far as possible in the form of a *Clinical Diary*. This diary, covering nine months (7 January to 2 October 1932), was certainly a step towards self-assertion and an attempt to understand all the depths of an analyst's position, without recourse to the dialogue and interaction of correspondence; nevertheless, the transference figure of Freud, the imagined addressee of this diary, can be clearly discerned. This diary is one of those rare books—one written by an analyst about himself. When an analyst reconsiders the whole of his life and work at such a depth of self-inquiry, this cannot be confined within the alternatives of orthodoxy or heterodoxy—however such terms are defined. The problem is stated on the first page: the "insensitivity of the analyst". We are in the midst of the subject: the analyst's "real countertransference", the need to know more about it, and the idea—almost in caricature—of "mutual" analysis.

In the case of R.N., Ferenczi "made the first effort to psychoanalyze countertransference in vivo" (Wolstein, 1989, p. 673), making this "a landmark case, a major turning point in the evolution of psychoanalytic therapy. It takes its place alongside those two other well-known failed cases in the history of psychoanalysis, Breuer's case of Anna O. and Freud's case of Dora" (p. 675). Countertransference is at issue—*negative* countertransference in particular. Ferenczi took up the lead where Freud had left it: Freud, instead using his "hate in the countertransference", as Winnicott was later to call it (Winnicott, 1947), as a *tool* in the treatment—as he had been able to do with positive and negative transference, and, to some extent, with positive countertransference—tended to discard patients who aroused negative feelings in him as being "unworthy" of analysis. In Ferenczi's concept, countertransference became an important tool, as did the analyst's weaknesses and errors: "One can almost say that the more an analyst shows weaknesses, which lead him to make greater or smaller mistakes, which can then be discovered and treated in mutual analysis, the better chance there is for the analysis to develop a deep and real basis" (Ferenczi, 1985 [1932], p. 15). The analyst's shortcomings also open the way to the deficiencies of the parents in the past: the emergence of analogous feelings may thus enhance a better understanding of the traumatizing effects of failures of the early environment, as mentioned before. The only other person in Freud's inner circle to study the positive uses of countertransference was Helene Deutsch (Deutsch, 1926), whose ideas were further developed by Heinrich Racker (1953, 1957). Later, Margaret Little's "rediscovery" of countertransference (Little, 1951, 1957), presented as the account of a situation between herself as analyst and a fictive patient, in fact originated, as she later revealed, in a situation when she as patient had felt hurt by an unempathic interpretation by *her own* analyst, Ella Freeman Sharpe (Little, 1990, p. 36). But the light thrown on countertransference has advantages for the analyst as well: "In one case this communication of my own mental state developed into a form of mutual analysis, from which I, the analyst, also derived considerable benefit" (p. 3). In experimenting with mutual analysis, Ferenczi went a step further still, though not without recognizing, after some time, its "dilemma" (p. 28), its dangers, and the limitations that restrict its use, finally coming to the conclusion: "Mutual analysis: only a last resort!" (p. 115).

If the idea of further exploring negative countertransference originated with Ferenczi, it was also due to the fact that he had experienced both roles, that of analyst and that of analysand, and who was sensitive—perhaps more than was Freud—toward the situation of the child, not only that of the adult. The child asks himself what the parents think about him and what the real motives of their behaviour are. This is the question of countertransference, and the basis of Ferenczi's speculation about Freud's inner position as an analyst, as he appears in the *Clinical Diary*.

CHAPTER FOUR

The history of
the concept of trauma:
Ferenczi at the end of the 1920s

In 1896, Freud emphasized the fact that "symptoms can only be understood if they are traced back to experiences that have a "traumatic" effect" and "they refer to the patient's sexual life. ... These sexual traumas must have occurred in early childhood (before puberty), and their content must consist of an actual irritation of the genitals" (Freud, 1896b, p. 163).

The Greek word "trauma" means injury. This first meaning already presents a perspective according to which we, the neurotic ones, are all injured, and this basic injury occurs in the area of sexuality—that is, in the area where our deepest, most visceral *desires*, desires that are with us continuously from the beginning of our existence, are *firmly rooted*. Later traumas arouse memory traces of earlier infantile traumas: these remain unconscious after the freeing of affect (especially anxiety) and after repression.

The important and well-known step in the history of that concept made by Freud in 1897 begins with the famous phrase: "I no longer believe in my neurotica" (F/Fl, 21.9.1897, Masson, 1985, p. 264). Having realized that the scenes of *seduction* were often invented by his patients, he introduced the idea that *traumas* were

43

linked to *fantasies* of desire: "The only impression we gain is that these events of childhood are somehow demanded as a necessity, that they are among the essential elements of a neurosis. If they have occurred in reality, so much to the good: but if they have been withheld by reality, they are put together from hints and supplemented by fantasy. The outcome is the same, and up to the present we have not succeeded in pointing to any difference in the consequences, whether it is fantasy or reality that has the greater share in these events of childhood. This sentence follows a remark of Freud's warning against underestimating the importance of *actual* seduction. In the context of recent discussions on this subject (especially following the publication of Masson's book in 1984), it seems important to point out that Freud's position does not imply the *negation of reality* of certain traumas, while acknowledging that others are formed by "allusions" ["*Andeutungen*"] completed by "fantasy" ["*durch die Fantasie ergänzt*"] ("Phantasie . . . oder . . . Realität den *grösseren* Anteil . . . hat", he writes—Freud, 1916–17, p. 370.)

The trauma, then, is situated at the level of an emerging *desire*, which comes up against the impossibility of its satisfaction, through the difficulties of realizing desires in the resistant material of "reality"—that is to say, the reality of the other. But this isn't all.

In another formulation, Freud asserts that: "A person only falls ill of a neurosis if his ego has lost the capacity to allocate his libido in some way ('die Libido unterbringen')" (Freud, 1916–17, p. 387). The ego feels helpless ("hilflos"—Freud, 1926d), abandoned to the situation, to a flood of *excitations too powerful* for the mental processes to deal with. In this sense the notion of trauma is essentially an economic concept (1916–17, p. 275)—a frustration in face of which the ego is helpless and overwhelmed.

The gross traumas of the period in which *Studies on Hysteria* (Freud, 1895d) and "Further Remarks on the Neuro-Psychoses of Defence" (Freud, 1896b) were written were often supplanted later on by more hidden and sometimes more insidious traumas. In the network of events, desires, and fantasies involved in this notion, the accent is put sometimes on one, sometimes on the other—according to the sensitivity of the analyst and the life and personal history of the analysand. The "abandonment" trauma of

Germaine Guex, René Spitz's hospitalization trauma, Bowlby's early separation, and others appear to depend on clear-cut economic and serious disruptions or discontinuities. Other traumas generate intrapsychic phenomena more subtly.

Trauma, then:

1. is linked to frustrated *desires*—the outcome of knowing whether or not there will be a trauma, will be determined at the point where an event meets with the images of a desire within the person ("the state of his ego"): the degree of his *helplessness;*

2. is clearly situated in the relationship with the *other*—the "drive object".

Hence the essential aspects of the problem concern the reality of the other, its *impact* on the psychic life of the subject, and the subject's capacities of *getting through* a trauma (his helplessness, his being overwhelmed).

In order to deal with these, let us recall that for Ferenczi it is the non-comprehension of adults, the "non-fitting", the non-correspondence, that is traumatic. These are the moments when the child is not understood, when he cannot *feel* understood. For the child seeking tenderness, the sexual aggression and passions of the adult create an acute situation of non-correspondence between two desires: those of the child and of the adult. This is only a beginning: subsequently, the child will feel split between what he has understood and what is said to him, between guilt and innocence, between simultaneous complicity and resistance. "Almost always the perpetrator behaves as though nothing had happened" (Ferenczi, 1933 [294], pp. 162–163). It is non-communication *after* the event that makes it really traumatic: it is in effect the *word* that makes it possible for the subject to overcome this "influx of excitation" that is trauma.

According to a presentation by Balint, who followed Ferenczi's work in London, the child is at first full of confidence. A second phase follows when the adult offers a "highly exciting, frightening or distressing experience" (Balint, 1969a, p. 432), an *intensive* interaction, but one that—he comments—is *not* "in itself traumatic". However, in a third phase, the child wants either to continue the game or to understand it and then comes up against a totally unexpected "refusal": the adult behaves as if he knew nothing at all about the earlier excitement; "he behaves as if nothing had happened" (p. 432).

Starting with this idea, Ferenczi's technique aimed at enabling the subject to relive ("to re-experience") the trauma and, through his *verbalization*, to achieve recall. For Ferenczi, in addition to *recall*, *repetition* in the transference and *experience* are fundamental elements of the psychoanalytic treatment, making a subsequent understanding possible. Freud recognized the importance of these ideas. For example, he regarded the book that Ferenczi and Rank co-authored in 1924 as a "corrective" to "his conception of the role of repetition and acting-out in analysis", which he had "viewed with fear" (Freud & Abraham, 1965a). Those incidents that they regarded as experiences appear to him as regrettable setbacks. He came to understand that Rank and Ferenczi drew attention to the fact that "living such experiences is inevitable and useful" (Freud & Abraham, 1965a).

Ferenczi stressed the considerable importance of sexual trauma: "I obtained above all new corroborative evidence of my supposition that the trauma, especially the sexual trauma as the pathogenic factor, cannot be valued highly enough"—and he adds, not without irony: "Even children of very respectable, sincerely puritanical families, fall victim to real violence or rape much more often then one had dared to suppose. Either it is the parents who try to find a substitute gratification in this pathological way for their frustration or it is people thought to be trustworthy—such as relatives (uncles, aunts, grandparents), governesses or servants—who misuse the ignorance and innocence of the child. The immediate objection—that these are only sexual fantasies of the child, a kind of hysterical lying—is unfortunately made invalid by the important number of such confessions, for example of assaults upon children committed by patients actually in analysis" (Ferenczi, 1933 [294], p. 161).

However, he already foresaw various consequences of trauma: "Not only emotionally, but also *intellectually* [underlined in original], can the trauma bring to *maturity* [emphasis added] a part of the person. I wish to remind you of the typical "dream of the wise baby" described by me several years ago, in which a newly born child or an infant begins to talk—in fact, teaches wisdom to the entire family. The fear of the uninhibited, almost mad adult changes the child, so to speak, into a psychiatrist and, in order to become one and to defend himself against dangers coming from people without self-control, he must know how to identify himself completely with them" (p. 165).

He also talks about parents: "In addition to passionate love and passionate punishment, there is a third method of helplessly binding a child to an adult. This is the *terrorism of suffering* [underlined in original]. Children have the compulsion to put to rights all disorder in the family, to burden, so to speak, their own tender shoulders with the load of all others; of course, this is not . . . altruism, but is in order to be able to enjoy again the lost rest and the care and attention accompanying it" (Ferenczi, 1930 [291], pp. 165–166).

Surprising thoughts indeed! One would think they were the product of a contemporary analyst, were it not known that they date from around 1930. They clarify the phenomena of splitting, of "true self" and its wise and precocious enveloping "false self", all of which has a direct link with Ferenczi's manner of understanding the reality of trauma. There is no doubt that the bases of analysis is the *reality* of *points* of *major* impact in the *history* of the subject—in his truth.

The concept of trauma is also the conceptual bridge that connects events in the external reality of the subject with their consequences on his internal world and with their influence on unconscious expectations, with a crystallization of fantasies and an augmentation of their strength.

Let us not forget that the revalorization of the concept of trauma in the course of contemporary psychoanalysis is also the reopening of a very old dossier—at least as old as psychoanalysis itself—the link between external and internal reality, between the event and its consequences on the internal world. It is a difficult and complex problem and an embarrassing one, which makes it all the more easy to brush it aside. Yet the impact of reality and especially of certain events that can justifiably be called "outstanding" on the internal life and indeed on the fantasies is undeniable.

Freud strengthens us in our convictions. He writes that it is "nonsensical to say that one is practising psychoanalysis if one excludes from examination and consideration precisely these earliest periods ['*Urzeiten*']" (1939a, p. 72). In a letter to Ferenczi, written on 16 September 1930, he says:

> The outline of your new ideas on the traumatic fragmentation of psychic life seems very lively to me and possesses something of the characteristic qualities of "Thalassa". However, I feel that taking into consideration the extraordinary synthetic activity of the ego, one can hardly speak of trauma, without at the same time treating the reactive scarring. It is this that engenders what is visible for us—the traumas. We then must soon understand them from their implications.

Their implications—in other words, the analysis of these sequences of events—becomes, for Sándor Ferenczi, a vital task of the analyst. In a paper that appeared in the year after his death, in 1934, in the *Internationale Zeitschrift für Psychoanalyse* and which collates five notes written at different times between 1920 and 1932 under the title *Reflections on traumatism*, Ferenczi reports the dream of a patient:

> A young girl (child?) lies at the bottom of a boat, white and almost dead. Above her a huge man oppressing her with his face. Behind them in a boat a second man is standing, somebody well known to her, and the girl is ashamed that this man witnesses the event. The boat is surrounded by enormously high, steep mountains, so that nobody can see them from any direction except, perhaps, from an aeroplane at an enormous distance. (Ferenczi, 1934 [296], in: Ferenczi, 1938 [1920–1932] [308], pp. 241–242)

Ferenczi comments:

> The first part of the dream corresponds to a scene partly well known to us, partly reconstructed from other dream material, in which the patient as a child slides upwards astride the body of her father and with childish curiosity makes all sorts of discovery trips in search of hidden parts of his body, during which both of them enjoy themselves immensely . . . The scene on the deep lake reproduces the sight of the man no longer able to control himself and the thought of what people would say if they knew [represented by the second man in the dream]. . . . The feeling of utter helplessness and of being dead [expressed in the dream is completed with the image of] the depth of

unconsciousness, which makes the events inaccessible from all directions, at the most perhaps God in Heaven could see the happenings, or an airman flying very very far away, i.e. emotionally uninterested. (Ferenczi, 1934 [296], in: Ferenczi, 1938 [1920–1932] [308], pp. 241–242)

Further on, he remarks that "the mechanism of projection, as the result of the narcissistic split, is also represented in the displacement of the events from herself on to "a girl".

For Ferenczi, "the therapeutic aim of the dream analysis is the restoration of direct accessibility to the sensory impressions", in a deep regression—he even speaks of "trance"—which may go "as it were behind the secondary dream and brings about the reliving of the events of the trauma in the analysis" (p. 242). The quality of the analytic contact in this situation is of vital importance to him. It is a contact "which demands much tact. If the expectations of the patients are not satisfied completely, they awake cross or explain to us what we ought to have said or done." He adds that in these cases "the analyst must swallow a good deal and he must learn to renounce his authority as an omniscient being" (p. 242).

This quotation, in his condensed style, contains important remarks about the transferential authority of the analyst and his true position and about the importance of recognizing one's errors. Let us quote Balint (1934b, p. 314): "Ferenczi never forgot that in fact, psychoanalysis had been invented by a patient, and that the merit of the doctor lies precisely in accepting the guidance of the patient, and in wanting to learn a new technique of cure from him." It is not by chance that the expression "elasticity" also comes from one of Ferenczi's patients. . . .

His courage in examining painful events, marked by the defeat of libidinal aims, where destructive forces had taken the upper hand, led Ferenczi to self-interrogations—to problems, in other words, of countertransference. His *Clinical Diary* from the year 1932, recently published through the unremitting attention of Judith Dupont and her group (*Le Coq-Héron*), is a moving testimony of this (Ferenczi, 1985 [1932]).

His capacity to confront the trauma in himself enables Ferenczi to understand the trauma of others. In these traumatic situations of "helplessness" (Freud, 1926d), the role of language, the *words* of the other, become very important. The function of the mother as stimulus shield and protective filter, of her verbalization and the understanding it provides enables the child, at least to work through the trauma. In dealing with traumas in the analysis, this role falls to the psychoanalyst. An example from Ferenczi seems to me to illustrate this very well. I am quoting from his *Clinical Diary*, written in 1932:

> R.N.'s dream. . . . Dr. Gx. forces her withered breast into R.N.'s mouth. "It isn't what I need; too big, empty—no milk." The patient feels that this dream fragment is a combination of the unconscious content of the psyches of the analysand and the analyst. She demands that the analyst should "let himself be submersed," even perhaps fall asleep. The analyst's associations in fact move in the direction of an episode in his infancy (*száraz dajka* [dry nurse] affair, at the age of one year); meanwhile the patient repeats in dream scenes of horrifying events at the ages of one and a half, three, five, and eleven and a half, and their interpretation. The analyst is able, for the first time, to link *emotions* with the above primal event and thus endow that event with the feeling of a real experience. Simultaneously the patient succeeds in gaining insight, far more penetrating than before, into the reality of these events that have been repeated so often on an intellectual level. At her demand and insistence, I help her by asking simple questions that compel her to think. I must address her as if she were a patient in a mental hospital, using her childhood nicknames, and force her to admit to the reality of the facts, in spite of their painful nature. It is as though two halves had combined to form a whole soul. The emotions of the analyst combine with the ideas of the analysand, and the ideas of the analyst (representational images) with the emotions of the analysand; in this way the otherwise lifeless images become events, and the empty emotional tumult acquires an intellectual content. (Ferenczi, 1985 [1932], pp. 13–14).

The analysis is the place where the demons of traumas can be worked through, once they have been re-experienced and actualized, by the *word* expressing the *understanding* of the analyst, by the acceptance of him as the one who *leads* the subject to feel accepted himself, in an atmosphere of honesty and absolute authenticity. That is the vision of psychoanalysis according to Sándor

Ferenczi and his response to traumas which he himself suffered so intensely.

One of his compatriots and a contemporary, probably the greatest Hungarian poet of the twentieth century, expressed it in lines that are well known and often recited, even in the schools of Hungary. Let me quote, in this context, the poet Attila József, who, in analysis at that time, makes us feel a similar situation. He says:

> You have made me the child again
> without a trace of thirty years of pain.
> I cannot move away, whatever I do
> it is to you I am drawn, despite myself.
>
> . . .
>
> I have slept on the threshold
> far from a mother's arms
> hiding within myself, insane.
> Above, a vacant heaven;
> O sleep ! it's at your door that I am knocking.
> There are those who weep in silence
> Yet seem hard like me,
> Look: my love for you is of such strength
> That I can love myself, with you.
>
> [Attila József: *You have made me the child* . . .
> (1936, in József, 1956)]

Ferenczi took as serious and pursued to its ultimate conclusions Freud's teaching according to which man is, from birth, endowed with libido, the aim of which as Freud has shown, is to create links (Freud, 1923b, p. 45; 1925h, p. 239). Every important failure brought about by the breakdown of this tendency or, in Ferenczi's words, every "catastrophe" must have important repercussions: hence the trauma. Is this only a romantic vision of man? Even if German romanticism could influence Freud and Ferenczi to emphasize the hidden sides of man behind the rationality displayed in the foreground, it is most certainly in the psychoanalytic vision of man that the importance of his affectivity, *Eros* and *Thanatos*, his fantasies, become evident and central. The problem of trauma is situated exactly at the crossroads of these ideas.

Traumas: are we talking about one or many? If we take this question up again in the light of what has been said, it would appear useful to recall the scientific context in which Ferenczi worked. The author of "Thalassa"—fascinated by geology and palaeontology, as Freud was in technology—could not but be influenced by the theories current at that time, during which the "catastrophic" theory was predominant, only giving place little by little to the "gradual" theory, that is to say to an image of evolution in which the determining factor is no longer the single catastrophe but consists of multiple levels. . . . Similarly in the psychoanalytic conceptualization, the model of an outstanding event could prepare the way for the investigation of the complexity of successive events in the history of the subject, for a conception of multiple traumas or repetitive traumas, which Masud Khan (1963) referred to as "cumulative".

The professional life of analysts is riddled with such traumas. Ferenczi certainly suffered a trauma in his relationship with Freud, and that affected the whole psychoanalytic movement. I am thinking here of the difficulties between Freud and Ferenczi, to which I can only allude (see Haynal, 1987) and which should be further re-examined in the important correspondence between these two men. Let it suffice to say that a state of mind evolved in which fear for the survival of psychoanalytic doctrine cast its gloom over the need for free research where the right to disagree was overshadowed by personal considerations and the memory of human weaknesses. In the end it created an atmosphere heavy with mistrust in this fine group of pioneer psychoanalysts. However, without any possible doubt, the very profound human bonds between the two men—the dignity of Freud, and Ferenczi's attachment to his master—finally saved their relations. A feeling of solidarity prevailed, and the discord between them did not degenerate into hostility. This was not always the case with other members of the Committee, who felt themselves involved in the tensions.

What did Ferenczi derive from those experiences for himself and for the psychoanalytic movement? I would like to quote some testamentary lines of Ferenczi from a letter to Ernest Jones on 6 January 1930 (Masson, 1984): "What we must take out of this is the lesson that psychoanalysts in particular, more then has been the case up to now, should not allow scientific and technical divergences to degenerate into personal attacks"—a "lesson" that, I think, has lost none of its meaning. . . .

The genius of Hungarian culture has impressed the world through the music of Liszt and Bartók in their passions and the restraint of their expression. This same passion is there in Ferenczi. In him it is a passion for truth—an indomitable curiosity alongside a total honesty and a proud independence mixed with a very Budapest brand of mischievousness, which may well reconcile us with the great traumas, the profound sufferings, and the overwhelming enigmas of life.

CHAPTER FIVE

The countertransference
in the work of Ferenczi

I assume that most readers have already passed through the two stages through which all beginners go: the stage of enthusiasm at the unexpected increase in our therapeutic achievements and the stage of depression at the magnitude of the difficulties that stand in the way of our efforts. At whatever point in this development, however, each reader may happen to be, my intention today is to show that we have by no means come to the end of our resources for combating the neuroses, and that we may expect a substantial improvement in our therapeutic prospects before long (Freud, 1910d, p. 141).

Introduction

The countertransference dimension was not lacking in Freud's perception of therapeutic relations. Nor indeed could it have been, considering that one of his pioneering publications, on Anna O, is based on the account of Breuer, including that of his countertransference and panic (a caricature of an "*a posteriori* account"). It is difficult not to caricature the kinds of countertransference revealed by the first psychoanalytic cases, such as the erotic counter-transferences of male therapists towards young women and other prototypal situations from the early days of psychoanalysis. Apart from Anna O and Josef Breuer, we have Sabina Spielrein and Carl Gustav Jung, or Elma Pálos and Sándor Ferenczi, and hovering in the background in each case is Freud, in the capacity, one is tempted to say, of "supervisor".

As everyone knows, the word "countertransference" appears for the first time in an exchange of letters between Freud and Jung about the latter's feelings and acting out in relation to Spielrein; a year later it *entered* the domain of public *psychoanalytic* nomenclature. Later, Freud seldom mentions it explicitly, although it is implicit in his telephone metaphor (Freud, 1912e, p. 115), where he describes the analyst's sensitivity as a precious *instrument* in the perception of his analysand's unconscious. However, he remains faithful to his ideal of the (if possible, neutral) scientific *observer*—an ideal shared by many of his great successors, including Melanie Klein, who, for her part, was afraid that, if more attention were devoted to the countertransference dimension, the perspective might shift from the analysand to the analyst (Grosskurth, 1986, p. 449).

Freud's address to the Budapest Congress in 1918 (subsequently published in 1919 as "Lines of Advance in Psycho-Analytic Therapy") is an important declaration on analytic practice, which is at the same time regarded as his swan-song on the subject. He was subsequently to entrust these matters to Ferenczi and, a little later, also to Rank—while, incidentally, explicitly inviting the former several times to concern himself with the problem of "technique" (F/Fer, 28.1.1912). (Freud also enjoins Ferenczi not to leave "technique in Stekel's hands"—F/Fer, 28.1.1912.) Psychoanalysis was, after all, originally conceived as a psychotherapeutic treatment directed towards the *disappearance of the symptom* and hence of the patient's suffering. Gradually, in particular at the beginning of the 1920s, this initial focus on symptoms *gave way* to a consideration of the patient's suffering as a whole in connection with his or her *psychic structure*, economic equilibrium, or, in the language of the time, "*character*": "character analysis" was now taking the stage. As it happens, Freud was to put its chief protagonist, Wilhelm Reich, in charge of technical training at the Vienna Psychoanalytic Institute—the training, that is, of young analysts in psychoanalytic practice in *his* (Freud's) city. Reich's predecessor in this position was Helene Deutsch, who used the experience as the basis for her contribution (Deutsch, 1926) on the "occult" forces present in the exchange between unconsciouses (what Ferenczi calls the "dialogue of unconsciouses"—Ferenczi, 1985 [1932], 12 April 1932, p. 84)—a non-verbal communication, as we would put it today, in which she distinguishes fundamentally between countertransference by identification and countertransference by complementarity. This distinction was subsequently to be elaborated in the writings of her pupil, Heinrich Racker, especially after his emigration to Latin America, where, for reasons of geographical inevitability, his ideas were later to be deemed "Kleinian". The British—for instance Ella Sharpe (1921)—were by this time particularly alive to the (sometimes) harmful effect of the countertransference, an issue to be taken up again years later by Wilhelm Reich (1933). The notion of "counterresistance" was introduced by Glover in 1927.

"Character analysis" and the fundamental importance of the countertransference were already fully accepted by the time Ferenczi gave rein to his intuition—which had been present from his very first analytic publications and was indeed discernible in his pre-analytic work (see chapter one). The first years of Sándor Ferenczi's collaboration with Sigmund Freud—characterized by the composition of papers such as "Transitory Symptom-Constructions during the Analysis" (1912 [85]), "To Whom Does One Relate One's Dreams?" (1913 [105]), "A Little Chanticleer" (1913b [114]), "On Falling Asleep during Analysis" (1914 [139]), and "The 'Forgetting' of a Symptom and Its Explanation in a Dream" (1914b [145])—already bear witness to his keen perception of the central importance of analysand–analyst interaction, as well as of the role of introjection in the transference ("Introjection and Transference", 1909 [67]).

In the main body of his work, starting in the 1920s, Ferenczi laid the foundations for a new conception of analysis, thereby *de facto* becoming the originator of post-Freudian and post-modern psychoanalysis—that of Balint, Winnicott, Bion, Kohut, Thompson, and even Lacan and others. He did so in the scattered notes of the skeleton of a book, his unfinished *Clinical Diary* of 1932 (Ferenczi, 1985 [1932]), which has been familiar to us for some years now thanks to the efforts of Judith Dupont, Paris, in editing it for publication.

This new conception of analysis is fundamentally bound up with Ferenczi's experience of working with *seriously ill* patients, who would nowadays be diagnosed as borderlines or as latent psychotics with episodes of manifest psychosis, or even sufferers from the "new maladies of the soul"—pathologies of the kind that we encounter repeatedly in our own work as analysts today.

The Diary: *the analyst's sensitivity*

The *Diary* characteristically begins with the problem of the analyst's "insensitivity", which, to Ferenczi, is merely an extension of the parental insensitivity discussed in "Confusion of Tongues between Adults and the Child" (Ferenczi, 1933 [294]). If this note is struck in the very first chord of the overture, the reason is that, for Ferenczi, sensitivity is a fundamental instrument of the analytic process and of the analyst's participation in it—his organ of perception (Freud, 1912e). This sensitivity must be maintained and cared for, in contrast to an analytic attitude of "desperately rigid clinging to a theoretical approach" (Ferenczi, 1985 [1932], 7.1.1932, p. 1) and "artificiality". In this connection he mentions his patient, N.G., "who never tired of telling me about a teacher she found insufferable, who . . . always maintained a pedantic attitude" (p. 1)—she was, of course, using this metaphor as a reproach to her analyst, Ferenczi. The *Diary* continues with a discussion of the case of Dm.[1], with the famous kisses that occasioned Freud's denunciation of Ferenczi—just as she wanted the seductive father of her childhood to be denounced and punished. This repetition in the transference, which was so important for the development of Dm.'s treatment, would never have come to light had it been throttled by a "rigid

---

[1] According to information from Judith Dupont, Dm. can now be identified as Clara Thompson.

clinging to technique" (emphasis added), theoretically justified by the doctrine of "neutrality" (this term, which was never used by Freud, found its way into his *œuvre* by way of Strachey's translation). The overture already heralds the action of the drama, which concerns the need to fight for the analyst's *freedom* to give up his pseudo-scientific or pseudo-doctrinaire clinging. As Ferenczi was later to point out, that attitude offers the benefits of belonging to an élite and of acceptance by his peers, but the analyst also holds fast to it for reasons such as convenience:

> The advantages of following blindly were: (1) membership in a distinguished group guaranteed by the king, indeed with the rank of field marshal for myself (crown-prince fantasy). (2) One learned from him and from his kind of technique various things that made one's life and work more comfortable: the calm, unemotional reserve; the unruffled assurance that one knew better; and the theories, the seeking and finding of the causes of failure in the patient instead of partly in ourselves. The dishonesty of reserving the technique for one's own person, the advice not to let patients learn anything about the technique; and finally the pessimistic view, shared with only a trusted few, that neurotics are a rabble, good only to support us financially and to allow us to learn from their cases: psychoanalysis as a therapy may be worthless. (Ferenczi, 1985 [1932], 4.8.1932, p. 185)

Ferenczi immediately recognizes that it is not (or not only) his knowledge but his sensitivity and *sincerity* (authenticity) that will allow correct working *à deux* within a couple in which neither partner is superior or inferior. Human failings too will be an integral part of the *process*, partly through guilt feelings and making amends. He also writes that the more weaknesses an analyst has, the more likely it will be that the analysis will rest on profound and realistic foundations, because larger or smaller mistakes and errors will be uncovered and treated in the course of analysis (Ferenczi, 1985 [1932], 19.1.1932, p. 15).

The entire *Diary* tells of a structure to be erected by *two parties*, in which the analyst's contribution is the counterpart of the analysand's. Far from occupying the position of a scientific observer in a laboratory, the analyst becomes one of the principal subjects; his countertransference is no longer "counter" in the sense of "against", but "with", and may even *precede* the transference—as others have often rediscovered since Ferenczi, without quoting him and sometimes without even knowing that he had put forward and elaborated this idea as long ago as in 1932.

Of course, the analyst's sensitivity must be worked on analytically; it must be elaborated ("worked through") by the analyst's analysis—and, as far as possible, by his or her self-analysis. This realization came about via the long detour of an experiment with mutual analysis (*gegenseitige Analyse*: Fer/Grod, p. 46): in the context of the analytic process, analysis of the analyst by the analysand may lead on to the possibility of mutual analysis, an idea which, from the historical point of view, was not particularly Ferenczian in origin, having been practised long before by the pioneers of psychoanalysis among themselves. The paradigm is the sea voyage of Freud, Jung, and Ferenczi to America on the U.S.S. *George Washington* in August 1909; two other well-known examples, although the occasions and circumstances are different, are those of Carl Gustav Jung and Otto Gross, and Sándor Ferenczi and Georg Groddeck.

The tensions in an open, undefended analysis of this kind may increase to a considerable pitch, unleashing very powerful forces that can work like an explosion of atoms (Ferenczi, 1985 [1932], 10.1.1932, p. 5). This phrase resounds like a prophecy, a prediction, ahead of subsequent actual events. . . . The explosion of suffering connected with memories then leads Ferenczi to reconsider *trauma* and its consequences, the fragmentation of individuality, the outcome of aggressive forces[2] counteracted by the life instinct, which, in the context of the analysis of R.N.—Elizabeth Severn—he calls "Orpha", the organizing life instincts (12.1.1932, p. 9). And it was R.N.'s analysis that led Ferenczi to go beyond the mere acknowledgment of "artificiality in the analyst's behaviour" and to identify inclinations "to kill or torture patients", and, as a reaction against these, "overdone friendliness", politeness—"that is, the destruction of all hope of a real . . . countertransference" (17.1.1932, p. 11). "Mutual analysis", as Ferenczi calls it—what we would call analysis of the analyst in parallel with his analytic

---

[2] It is interesting to note that Ferenczi was occasionally prepared to interpret the death instinct as an instinct of self-sacrifice (Ferenczi, 1985 [1932], 26.4.1932, p. 91).

work—"will also be less terribly demanding, will promote a more genial and helpful approach in the patient, instead of the unremittingly all-too-good, selfless demeanor, behind which exhaustion, unpleasure, even murderous intentions are hidden" (19.1.1932, p. 16).

R.N.'s dream, quoted above, calls into question the exaggerated demands of the analytic *superego*. If the analyst gets an insight into his/her weaknesses, he may also abandon his excessive expectations of indulgence. Ferenczi realizes that he cannot guarantee the analysand complete and life-long happiness when he feels himself partly as a child—that is to say, in need of care.[3]

Everything takes place in interaction and intersubjectivity, in the subjectivity of the analysand and of the analyst. Thus, when he felt tired, he could leave the patient for quite a long time "undisturbed" in her relaxed state, whereas at other times he had the habit—with some patients in particular—of engaging in conversations from which the analysands sometimes defended themselves with an energetic "shut up" (Ferenczi, 1985 [1932], 4.2.1932, p. 29)—as in the marvellous Budapest story: a man in debt answers persecutory telephone calls from his creditor by exclaiming: "What a wonderful invention the telephone is! You can hear every word!"

Even the analyst's answers *are* sometimes "beside the point"; however, every one of his words is heard, as is, through this exchange, the reflection of the transference–countertransference situation—that is, the *interaction*, or, in other words, the communication between the two protagonists.

Communication

After all, if the processes of unconscious communication are no longer blocked, the result may sometimes be a kind of flow from one party to the other—in effect, a *Gedankenübertragung* or thought transference (Ferenczi, 1985 [1932], 14.2.1932, p. 33). This also pre-

---

[3] Once the exaggerated demands have been reduced, the "end result of the analysis of transference and countertransference may be the establishment of a kind, dispassionate atmosphere, such as may well have existed in pretraumatic times" (Ferenczi, 1985 [1932], 31.1.1932, p. 27).

supposes an "ability to relax" on the part of the analyst at this particular time. For Ferenczi, this ability was considerably limited because of the very early memories of a rough treatment received from a nurse after an incident of anal soiling. This gave rise to overestimation of the wishes, likes, and dislikes of other people, accompanied by some dramatic slips like spilling coffee or water. These were on occasion revealed in his countertransference. In R.N. he thought he found his mother again—someone hard and energetic, of whom he was afraid. R.N. knew this and treated him very gently. *Past and present* intermingle in the countertransference, by which some of the analysand's reactions are in turn determined. Delving more deeply into the matter, Ferenczi is finally led

> to realize that this is an unavoidable task for the analyst: although he may behave as he will, he may take kindness and relaxation as far as he possibly can, the time will come when he will have to repeat with his own hands the act of *murder* previously perpetrated against the patient. In contrast to the original murder, however, he is not allowed to deny his guilt. (Ferenczi, 1985 [1932], 8.3.1932, p. 52, emphasis added)

This repeats a "tragic moment" in Sándor's childhood, when his mother declared: "You are my murderer" (p. 53). Back in his analyses, he recognizes that if "one knows that this hangman's work is inevitable, that in the end it does help the patient", then "one overcomes the resistance against such cruelty, which can vary in strength"; and "one will not shrink . . ." (p. 53). The concomitant interweaving of transference and countertransference gives "the impression of two equally terrified children who compare their experiences, and because of their common fate understand each other completely and instinctively try to comfort each other" (13.3.1932, p. 56).

The memory of infantile events guides Ferenczi on to

> the image of a corpse, whose abdomen I was opening up, presumably in the dissecting room; linked to this the mad fantasy that I was being pressed into this wound in the corpse. Interpretation: the after-effect of passionate scenes, which presumably did take place, in the course of which a housemaid probably allowed me to play with her breasts, but then pressed my head between her legs, so that I became frightened and felt

I was suffocating. This is the source of my hatred of females: I want to dissect them for it, that is, to kill them. That is why my mother's accusation "You are my murderer" cut to the heart and led to (1) a compulsive desire to help anyone who is suffering, especially women; and (2) a flight from situations in which I would have to be aggressive. ... Thus ... exaggerated reactions of guilt at the slightest lapse. (Ferenczi, 1985 [1932], 17.3.1932, p. 61)

The exemplary attempt to become acquainted with the feelings and reactions activated by analysands makes it possible to identify the profound nature of the interaction and to understand analysands' feelings of dependence, reparation, and gratitude toward the analyst. Ferenczi finally asks how much *Mitgefühl*—sympathy or "feeling with"—the analyst must have (p. 60).

Should it ... occur, as it does occasionally to me, that experiencing another's and my own suffering brings a tear to my eye (and one should not conceal this emotion from the patient), then the tears of doctor and of patient mingle in a sublimated communion, which perhaps finds its analogy only in the mother–child relationship. And this is the healing agent, which, like a kind of glue, binds together permanently the intellectually assembled fragments, surrounding even the personality thus repaired with a new aura of vitality and optimism. (Ferenczi, 1985 [1932], 20.3.1932, p. 65)

This sublimated *communion*, also made up of mutual identification, is utilized once more, opening up the possibility of a "new beginning" of the kind that was to become dear to Michael Balint.

It is only when [a] grafted-on element is re-experienced in analysis, and is thereby emotionally split up, that there develops *in the analysis*, initially in the transference relationship, that *untroubled* infantile sexuality from which, in the final phase of analysis, the longed-for [state] will grow. (Ferenczi, 1985 [1932], 31.3.1932, p. 75)

Let us pause at this sentence, first of all to demonstrate clearly to those who fear the disappearance of infantile sexuality in this intersubjectivity *à la* Ferenczi, which is based on the understanding first and foremost of the countertransference, that on the contrary, infantile sexuality emerges as a clearly defined objective of the analysis. Here we are in effect already hearing some of the reservations occasionally voiced today: Ferenczi adds (in his note of 5.4.1932): "The fact that infantile sexuality exists obviously remains undisputed" (p. 79). (However, he leaves open the question of "how much of the Oedipus complex is really inherited and how much is passed on by tradition from one generation to the other"— Ferenczi, 1985 [1932], 5.4.1932, p. 79.)

The analyst in question

In parallel with the discovery of the importance of the countertransference, Ferenczi also assigns it a place in the *history* of psychoanalysis.

> I tend to think that originally Freud really did believe in analysis; he followed Breuer with enthusiasm and worked passionately, devotedly, on the curing of neurotics (if necessary spending hours lying on the floor next to a person in a hysterical crisis). He must have been first shaken and then disenchanted, however, by certain experiences, rather like Breuer when his patient had a relapse and when the problem of countertransference opened up before him like an abyss. (Ferenczi, 1985 [1932], 1.5.1932, p. 93 [*wie ein Abgrund sich öffnenden Gegenübertragung*: German edition, p. 142])

Again, "what we call the transference situation is actually not a spontaneous manifestation of feelings in the patient, but is created by the analytically produced situation, that is, artificially created by the analytic technique" (Ferenczi, 1985 [1932], 3.5.1932, p. 95). Hence, "if the doctor does not watch himself, he will remain longer than necessary in this situation, comfortable for him, in which his patients spare him the unpleasure of self-criticism and give him the opportunity to enjoy his superiority, and to be loved . . ." (p. 93). "Certain of the doctor's theories (delusions) may not be challenged; if one does so nevertheless, then one is a bad pupil . . ., one is in a state of resistance" (p. 94). (What a problematic judgement this is, even if we are all prepared to accept that this phenomenon does exist in analytic treatment. The problem lies in the fact that it is the analyst who *declares* what material is a resistance, often totally subjectively.)

The analyst should therefore "be openly a human being with feelings, empathic at times and frankly exasperated at other times" (p. 94). ". . . there is thus a better and quicker prospect of sinking back into the traumatic past, and from this a recovery can be expected that will be definitive, spontaneous, and no longer based on authority" (p. 94). "As for the doctor, thus sobered from his scientific delusion" (p. 94), because clinging to theory may (in the analyst's personal economy) be virtually a delusion, he can begin to "acquire possibilities for enjoying life" (p. 95). However, it is also possible for the analyst to overdo his expectation of transference manifestations. The interpretation of every detail as expressing an affect towards the analyst—which Ferenczi recognises he may, with Rank, have exaggerated—is, moreover, likely to produce a kind of paranoid atmosphere that an objective observer could describe as a narcissistic, egocentric, and sometimes erotomaniacal delusion of the analyst: me, me, me. . . . In these cases, one is all too inclined to assume too quickly that the patient either is in love with us or hates us—though the situation is sometimes more complex.

Ferenczi describes the snares of the satisfaction of being admired by patients and placed in a position of superiority. R.N. frightens him by casting him in the role of the "perfect lover" (5.5.1932, p. 98). He discovers his fear of powerful female figures. On the other hand, however, he describes the stimulation obtained from his (male or female) analysand(s), a phenomenon consistent with "having (or having been) woken up" (*Aufgewecktsein*, German edition, p. 152) by the influence of the male or female patient (8.5.1932, p. 102): the analysand can mobilize the analyst's interest in a kind of "mutual seduction". "At this critical moment my 'having (or having been) woken up' then appears to have intervened" (p. 102).

Ferenczi recommends talking about the analyst's own feelings in certain circumstances. He describes how, in "the wake of a 'psychoanalytic confession'" (the disclosure of his dislike of a homosexual relationship), the analysand has the "feeling of colossal triumph and self-assurance never experienced before: So I was right after all!" Ferenczi reports that this kind of analytical experience enables the patient to reach a much stronger conviction of the reality of certain events from his/her childhood, which, in turn, triggers a nightmare. Such self-revelation raises nevertheless the problem of determining how far neutrality can be maintained in such circumstances and to what extent the lack of disclosure would border on hypocrisy.

Ferenczi says that this was the point at which their paths diverged, and he began to question certain suppositions in psychoanalytical technique. He began to examine errors. He then thought that he had gone too far in seeing transference everywhere. He tried to pursue the Freudian technique of frustration "honestly and sincerely" to the end in his active therapy. Following its failure, he attempted "permissiveness and relaxation", which, in the *Clinical Diary*, he considers again as an exaggeration. In the wake of what he considers two defeats and as a result of what he learned from all these experimentations, he seems to have found his personal style reflected in his *Diary*. Nevertheless, it is true that during her analysis, Dm. (Clara Thompson) still had the courage to reproach him that at the first signs of incomplete adaptation or submission analysts abandon their pupils.

R.N.—who, it should be remembered, was the initiator of one of Ferenczi's two mutual analyses—claims that Ferenczi was "the only person in the world who owing to his special personal fate could and would make amends for the injury that had been done to her" (Ferenczi, 1985 (1932), 4.8.1932, p. 121). Ferenczi adds that this capacity for reparation was discovered in the course of their mutual analysis—that is, that he was able to understand his capacity to "make amends" to analysands in consequence of his sense of guilt because of the death of his sister, Vilma, two years his junior, who had died of diphtheria. This bore out his conviction that the analyst depends on his feelings and can succeed only if he really does love the patient. However, he observes: "It is true that as a doctor one is tired, irritable, somewhat patronizing, and now and then one sacrifices the patient's interests to one's own curiosity, or even half-unconsciously makes covert use of the opportunity to give vent to purely personal aggression and cruelty" (p. 130). In this way, we fail to place ourselves at the patient's disposal in "a passionately active manner"—as Ferenczi says (p. 130). Having grasped the mutual links, he is able to write: "Special task: to free the patients whom psychoanalytic paranoia has reduced to the status of

minors[4], made dependent and permanently attached, truly to liber-
ate them, *from us as well*" (19.7.1932, p. 161; emphasis in original).

> The way in which psychoanalysis operates in the relationship
> between doctor and patient must impress the latter as
> deliberate cruelty. One receives the patient in a friendly man-
> ner, works to establish transference securely, and then, while
> the patient is going through agonies, one sits calmly in the
> armchair, smoking a cigar and making seemingly conventional
> and hackneyed remarks in a bored tone; occasionally one falls
> asleep. (Ferenczi, 1985 [1932], 27.7.1932, p. 178)

Latent sadism and "erotomania" in the analyst

> I do not know of any analyst whose analysis I could declare,
> theoretically, as concluded (least of all my own). Thus we have,
> in every single analysis, quite enough to learn about ourselves.
> Analysis offers to persons otherwise somewhat incapacitated
> and whose self-confidence and potency are disturbed an op-
> portunity to feel like a sultan, thus compensating him for his
> defective ability to love. Analyzing this condition leads to a
> salutary loss of illusions about oneself and thus to the awaken-
> ing of a real interest in others. If one has overcome one's narcis-
> sism in this way, one will soon acquire that sympathy and love
> of humanity without which the analysis is just a protracted
> vexation. (Ferenczi, 1985 [1932], 8.8.1932, p. 194)

On 13 August 1932, Ferenczi compiles a "catalogue of the sins" of
psychoanalysis based on the reproaches of a woman patient. The
upshot of this is that the analyst does not succeed in solving certain
problems if he doesn't know himself sufficiently and is accordingly
not able to adopt an appropriate attitude (13.8.1932, p. 199). Ferenczi fears that otherwise we would be immersed in "the *endlessness*
of the traumatic repetitions (six to eight years long!)" (p. 200),

---

[4]This reading is the same as that of the French translation and suggests that
Ferenczi used the word *unmündig*; however, the published German version (p.
219) has the word *unwürdig*, so that the meaning would be "whom psychoanalytic paranoia has deprived of their dignity".

because the repetition of the past is always experienced as occurring in the present and because the trauma cannot be resolved and overcome in the repetition of transference mechanisms. "Without sympathy there is no healing, but at most an insight into the genesis of the patient's suffering (Ferenczi, 13.8.1932, p. 200); this clearly shows that an experience—an affective exchange—is held by Ferenczi, beyond insight, to be an important factor of change. However, he also notes: "Kindness alone would not help much either, but only *both together* [intellectual dissection and kindness]" (17.8.1932, p. 207, emphasis added).

As to the consequences of countertransference attitudes, Ferenczi takes as an example Freud's attitude toward women patients because of his "unilaterally androphile orientation of his theory of sexuality". Almost all of his pupils, Ferenczi included, followed him on this path. In his *Clinical Diary* he therefore comes to the conclusion that a new edition of his theory of genitality "would mean complete rewriting".

When, in the situation of interaction and intersubjectivity, the sky begins to darken, the analyst makes mistakes, and his ability to understand declines, the analysis approaches the area of traumatization. The confusion in the analyst–analysand relationship shows that an old confusion, an old *Sprachverwirrung* or confusion of tongues, is being repeated and a trauma relived. And it is only through this trauma, through the analyst's mistakes and his annihilation of the analysand, that, according to Ferenczi, the analysis can truly succeed in changing the past with a view to the future. A new experience—a kind of new beginning—thus becomes possible.

Conclusions

A dichotomy can be established between, on the one hand, Freud, the scientist, inclining toward exact knowledge, insight and mastery—"Where id was, there ego shall be" (Freud, 1933a, p. 80)—and, on the other hand, contemporary psychoanalysis, ushered in by Ferenczi, who questions the psychoanalytic notions created by the analytic situation, who contributes to it (whether intentionally or not) by his silences or claimed neutrality—his abstention, in other words—and who tries to accompany the suffering human being to the furthermost possible limits in such a situation. Whereas Freud followed in the footsteps of the *Aufklärung*, the German Enlightenment, emphasizing human *liberation* through *rational knowledge*, Ferenczi belongs more in the romantic tradition, stressing as he did the *personal*, individual and *subjective*, what takes place first and foremost in "I–Thou" encounters (Martin Buber). Taking the view that the analyst is responsible for "maintaining" the patient, in Winnicott's (later) sense of "holding", Ferenczi even allowed himself to hold the patient physically or, as the caricature of Balint has it, at least to allow the little fingers of analyst and patient to touch. For Freud, interpretation is ultimately the only way of touching the other through his insight—that is, his rationality. To Fenichel, in this Freudian position, Freudism was the rational science of the irrational. Ferenczi believed that irrational intuitions could also *touch* the subject. With Ferenczi, this light, empathic touch is called *tact*. When Winnicott was once asked how to adapt to patients' needs with the flexibility he advocated, he is said to have answered that one ought perhaps not to treat more than one patient at a time. When we observe Ferenczi going to patients' homes, seeing some of them twice a day, seeing them on Saturdays, Sundays, and during his vacations, we might well say that he tried to achieve this "rhythm of the impossible". In his obituary, Freud said that Ferenczi had gone to the "limit" of the psychoanalysis of his day, beyond the call of the devotion that he himself and many Freudians deemed judicious, reasonable, or appropriate. Whereas Freud held that in education, whatever one did one was bound to be wrong, and that somewhere the work of the death instinct and other limitations, such as the limits of sexual pleasure or the constraints of civilization, imposed such a burden on man that it was difficult to overcome the discontents inherent in our civilization, Ferenczi thought that self-realization and authenticity between individuals ought to be achievable (see Fer/F, 5.2.1910, 14.2.1913, etc.). Freud advocated the abandonment of illusions—such as, for example, religion—while Ferenczi, and later Winnicott, pleaded in favour of play, of creative activity, including artistic creation, which is, after all, ultimately illusory. Freud saw the vicissitudes of the drives, whereas Ferenczi was more concerned with the individual's achievements resulting from the same drives. The environment for Freud was hostile and man's self-realization fragile; for Ferenczi, on the other hand, the environment offered prospects for development, especially in psychoanalytic therapy. For Michel Foucault, as for Sándor Ferenczi, individuality was an artistic achievement; whereas for Freud, life was a process marked by suffering. Even if Freud surely shared Goethe's idea of realizing one's full potential—*sei der Du bist* [be who thou art], its full flowering was to be left to Ferenczi.

We have, then, an antagonism between an anonymous, impassive observer working by a virtually impersonal set of rules and an analyst not averse to self-disclosure who believes that, whether one likes it or not, one is always bound to give oneself away.

While asserting that people always project into something that is already present ("The jealousy of the second layer, *projected* jealousy, is derived in both men and women either from their own actual unfaithfulness in real life or from impulses towards it which have succumbed to repression. . . . Anyone who denies these temptations in himself . . . can obtain this alleviation—and, indeed, acquittal by his conscience—if he projects his own impulses to faithlessness. . . ."—Freud, 1922b, p. 224), Freud implies that the contributions of the analyst act as crystallization points in determining the nature of the projections.

Epilogue

Here we find Ferenczi working with the countertransference, which is seen as a composite entity made up of psychic elements contributed by both analyst and analysand, a creation not of one or of the other, but of *both*, which must be analysed in its *complexity*, in the knowledge that there can be no direct access to the unconscious without the effort of analysis.

What is new and original in Ferenczi's approach to the problem of the countertransference is that it is a personal one, a play of the "I", which betrays his experiences, questionings, uncertainties, and doubts, as well as, at the same time, his devotion to his analysands and to the cause of psychoanalysis. This unique attitude marks the beginning of a new form of analysis, which fulfils the "mission" entrusted to him by Freud's repeated injunctions to concern himself with psychoanalytic "technique" (see, for example, F/Fer, 28.1.1912). He made the practice of analysis different from Freud's. Although Freud had difficulty in following ideas and issues that were no longer under his control, this trend nevertheless originated with him, for he was more intuitive and more inspired with genius than the scientistic formulae with which he tried to master later developments might suggest. By returning to the theme of trauma and catharsis, and hence to *experience* in the analytic situation, Ferenczi was going back to a younger Freud—one who had not yet lost his enthusiasm. By rethinking the analytic situation from the point of view of the *analyst*, he paved the way for later workers who set off in the same direction and laid the foundations of the contemporary, postmodern, post-Freudian psychoanalysis that has characterized analytic practice in the second half of the twentieth century. And by directing the analyst's sensitivity towards what takes place between him or her and the analysand, including the analyst's contribution to the analytic situation, he shifted the focus of psychoanalysis away from reconstruction and intellectual understanding of the past onto an interpersonal experience centring on what is repeated and remembered; in this way he took up Freud's ideas from the point they had reached in 1914 with "Remembering, Repeating and Working-Through" (Freud, 1914g).

Ferenczi's examination of the countertransference enabled him to make some fundamental discoveries, as it were, incidentally. These concerned, for example, infantile sexuality, as well as such other matters as toleration of being alone (Ferenczi, 1985 [1932], 8.8.1932, pp. 191–193), identification with the aggressor (7.8.1932, p. 190), and the relief to which the suicide may aspire (30.7.1932, p. 180), to mention only a few.

I cannot end this chapter without pointing out that neither Ferenczi nor, for that matter, Balint ever wanted to found a school, because they had no wish to recreate an infantilizing situation that might deprive the analyst of his own responsibility, sensitivity, and creativity. In my view, Ferenczi's importance can be correctly understood if we see him within the line of those who have investigated the unconscious aspects of man and of the resulting aspirations to help him—in other words, Freudian theory and technique. Ferenczi should not be regarded as having solved every problem, even if he did point the way towards authentic consideration of the issues of interaction in a field comprising the analyst and the analysand. Without de-idealizing him to some extent, there can be no progress; and without de-idealizing him, we are liable to end up again in the realm of a good/bad antithesis, in which, this time, he is the goodie and others—sometimes including Freud—are the baddies. Hence my personal rejection of the phrase "humanistic psychoanalysis" when applied to Ferenczi—as if Freud and others in the psychoanalytic movement had not been humanists. Justice cannot be done to the complexity and fertility of the psychoanalytic enterprise and its immense liberating potential without also taking account of the difficulties inherent both in its practice and in theorizing about that practice. Ferenczi shows us a way, but this does not mean that we should idealize him and regard him as the only psychoanalytic thinker. All the same, he must surely be deemed one of the masters in the historical context of the evolution and maturation of ideas on psychoanalytic practice and in that of the contemporary post-classical enterprise. There is no such thing as definitive knowledge, but only questioning and searching for the way forward, and in this respect Ferenczi is one of the undisputed mentors of our generation, as he was of its predecessors.

We must not allow Ferenczi's legacy to assume the structure of a sect; he himself would have abhorred such a trend. Knowledge about Ferenczi, as Judith Vida (1996) put it, should fecundate the whole of the psychoanalytic movement and allow it to advance in such a way as to improve the treatment of our patients and analysands, as Ferenczi would have wished.

CHAPTER SIX

Slaying the dragons of the past or cooking the hare in the present: a historical view on affects in the psychoanalytic encounter

W hile we would all agree that transference is of central importance to psychoanalytic treatment, it remains a matter of continuing controversy as to how much and in what ways the phenomena described with this term are to be attributed to present "reality" or to past "illusion". In his earliest formulations, Freud tied these affective manifestations to the patient's *past*. However, this view—which may in retrospect be seen as covertly containing a distancing manoeuvre included for the comfort of the analyst—did not represent a satisfactory or definitive *solution* to all of the difficulties present. Ultimately, Freud developed a complex position: on the one hand, he continued to see transference feelings as "new editions" of old "facsimiles" (Freud, 1905e [1901], p. 116); on the other, he not only acknowledged the actuality of these feelings but saw them as an important tool for change within the treatment.

The nature of the actual, on-going interactions between analysand and analyst and the feelings and experience that these gave rise to later became the subject of intense investigation and lively exchange between Freud and members of his circle. Ferenczi, in particular, assumed a leading role in expanding upon Freud's original ideas. While some of Ferenczi's innovative concepts—such as a deepened appreciation of the interactive dimension of the analytic relationship, the fundamental importance of the *analyst's feelings* as a tool for understanding the evolution of the psychoanalytic process, and the role of the mother in determining the transference—were accepted by an important part of the psychoanalytic community, often without explicit acknowledgement of their origin, others, such as mutual analysis and the revival of child-hood trauma during analysis, were disparaged or rejected. This followed, among others, as a consequence of Freud's ambivalence and the opposition of important members of his environment (e.g. Karl Abraham and Ernest Jones) towards some of these ideas. Over time, however, Ferenczi's ideas have progressively resurfaced in contemporary descriptions and theories of the therapeutic encounter. It therefore seems appropriate for me to attempt to trace these ideas back to their origin and examine, in the historical context, their early elaboration and the conflicts that have surrounded them almost from their inception. In doing so, I hope to create a context that will allow my readers to appreciate the complexities of these issues and their importance for the psychoanalytic community as a whole.

In considering his early psychotherapeutic experiences, Freud wrote that "it is almost inevitable that [the patients'] relation to [the therapist] will force itself . . . unduly into the foreground" (Freud, with Breuer, 1895d], p. 266), and that this relationship can even become "the worst obstacle that we can come across" (p. 301). But it cannot be avoided because one "can . . . reckon on meeting it in every comparatively serious analysis" (p. 301).

Freud already felt that he was working in the shade of affects: the "procedure . . . presupposes . . . personal concern for the patients. . . . I cannot imagine bringing myself to delve into the psychical mechanism of a hysteria in anyone who . . . would not be capable of arousing human *sympathy*" (p. 265; emphasis added). Moreover, this sympathy is also *demanded* by the patients—who view their cooperation as "a personal sacrifice, which must be compensated by some substitute for love" (p. 301).

Yet, very early, Freud encountered love not only in this mild "substitute" form, but also in its full affective implications—

thus becoming a disturbance. In this context let me evoke his well-known report, according to which a patient "threw her arms around my neck" and only the "unexpected entrance of a servant relieved us from a painful discussion" (1925d [1924], p. 27). A proof of *love*, it seems, about the motives of which Freud pondered, however: "I was modest enough not to attribute the event to my own irresistible personal attraction" (p. 27), but to the *past* of the subject. In linking the patients' emotions with the past, he saw them as a *"false connection"* (1895d, p. 302) and thus came to conceptualize the notion of *transference*. (A year earlier, Freud [1894a, p. 52] had described obsessional neurosis and phobia in using the same expression: "false connection" ["transfer" in Greek: *metaphor* = transfer of sense; "transfer" in the psychoanalytical meaning is a metaphor—transfer of sense].)

As far as his own reaction to the theme of sexuality is concerned, we find that remarkable report in *The Psychopathology of Everyday Life* that "a young girl . . . aroused a feeling of pleasure in me which I had long thought was extinct." By an "apparently clumsy movement", he continues, "I suddenly found myself standing directly behind her, and throwing my arms round her from behind; and for a moment my hands met in front of her waist" (1901b, p. 175; "In front of her waist" is an attenuated translation by Alan Tyson in the *Standard Edition* of the original German "vor ihrem Schoss" [GW 4, p. 195]—the usual euphemism for the female genitals).

In the discussion of the Dora case he confessed his vulnerability: "No one who, like me, conjures up the most evil of those half-tamed demons that inhabit the human breast, and seeks to wrestle with them, can expect to come through the struggle unscathed" (Freud, 1905e [1901], p. 109). This case has, in recent years, received much attention and has been subject to historical and psychoanalytical re-evaluation (cf. Decker, 1991; Jennings, 1986). In my opinion it is here that Freud fully recognized his failure of not having considered *affective implications*, writing: "I was deaf to this first note of warning" (Freud, 1905e [1901], p. 119). We can only speculate, as Decker (1991) does, that Freud might have been sexually aroused by this young woman, who spoke to him about her sexual temptations during the treatment. In any case, to conceal his embarrassment, he found it necessary to make an apologetic explanation in a foreign language about being able to discuss sexual matters with a young lady: *"J'appelle un chat un chat"* ["I call a cat a cat"] (1905e [1901], p. 48), and: *"Pour faire une omelette il faut casser des oeufs"* ["To make an omelette you have to break eggs"] (p. 49).[1] Freud evidently took a parental stance and recognized that it was again "transference" that led to the failure of the treatment. Unsettled by this case, he wrote it up at one go, in a burst of impassioned enthusiasm, between 10 and 25 January 1901, breaking off work on *The Psychopathology of Everyday Life* (Freud, 1901b); and afterwards, by various contradictory actions, he delayed its publication for four years.

But Freud was also implicated in other experiences of over-involvement, related to him by his closest collaborators and friends: Josef Breuer, Carl Gustav Jung, and Sándor Ferenczi.

. . . with Breuer . . .

The first of these incidents where love was triggered in the therapeutic situation, was transformed to passion, and obviously could not be mastered was that between Anna O, Josef Breuer, and Freud himself. Even if this encounter was to become, later on, the object of legend (Breuer breaking off the treatment in panic and leaving with his wife for a second honeymoon to Venice, there procreating his last child), the whole affair was, without any doubt, unsettling enough (cf. Hirschmüller, 1978, pp. 170–178)[2]. All this seemed so important to Freud that he did not hesitate to declare in the opening phrases of the first of the Clark lectures that the "merit to have

---

[1] See also Freud's turning to Spanish as an "official language" (Freud, 1989, p. 11) in his adolescent letters to Silberstein—at a point, when he is going to write about his highly emotionally charged relationship with Gisela Fluss—just as in his first description of oedipal feelings to Fliess (3.10.1897; in Masson, 1985, p. 268) he had recourse to the Latin "matrem . . . nudam".

[2] Cf. Freud's (F/SZw, 2.6.1932; in Zweig, 1989, p. 162) and Jones's (1953, pp. 246–7) reconstruction of the affair. It is interesting, by the way, that Freud chose as pseudonym for his patient Ida Bauer (*Fragment of an Analysis of a Case of Hysteria* (1905e [1901]) the name Dora (cf. Decker 1991), the very name of Breuer's last child, conceived *during* his treatment of Bertha Pappenheim.

brought psycho-analysis into being" (Freud, 1910a [1909], p. 9) had to be attributed to Dr Breuer and to his patient (Bertha Pappenheim).

Josef Breuer, for his part, in recalling the case of Anna O, wrote in a letter to Auguste Forel on 21 November 1907, that he had "learned . . . that a "general practitioner [in English in the German text] cannot treat such a case without being totally destroyed in his activities and life style. I have sworn by that time that I will never go through such an ordeal again" (Ackerknecht, 1957, p. 170; translated for this edition).

Decades later, writing his *Clinical Diary*, Ferenczi recalled the beginning of Freud's clinical practice and his dislike of regressive phenomena as a problem of countertransference. Ferenczi attributed this difficulty to Freud's discovery that hysterics lie. He thought that since making this discovery, Freud no longer loved his patients.

After the triangular situation with Breuer, Anna O, and himself, Freud was to find himself—as far as we know—involved in similar situations in transference-triggered love affairs on two more occasions, at least: in that between Sabina Spielrein and Carl Gustav Jung (1908–09) and, a few years later, in that between Elma Pálos and Sándor Ferenczi (1911–12).

. . . with Jung . . .

The correspondence between Freud and Jung begins, as in an antique drama, with a seemingly insignificant statement, which is nevertheless a sign of future trouble: "I am currently treating an hysteric with your method", writes Jung. "Difficult case, a 20-year-old Russian girl student, ill for 6 years" (Ju/F, 23.10.1906). It is only three years later, in 1909, that the real "incident" occurring in the story with Sabina Spielrein is brought up by Jung, in a very hypocritical manner: "A woman patient, whom years ago I pulled out of a very sticky neurosis with unstinting effort, has violated my confidence and my friendship in the most mortifying way imaginable. She has kicked up a vile scandal solely because I denied myself the pleasure of giving her a child." He insists—falsely—that "I have always acted the gentleman towards her", but at the same time speaks of having discovered his "polygamous components" (Ju/F, 7.3.1909). . . .

Already in 1906, Freud had recognized, in a letter to Jung, that analysis is "actually a healing through love" (6.12.1906; p. 13; translated for this edition), and he repeated this a month later at a meeting of the Vienna Psychoanalytic Society (30.1.1907; Nunberg & Federn, 1962, p. 101).[3] On 19 January 1908, he wrote to Abraham: "Back to technique.[4] You are right, that was the most taxing of all to acquire, and that is why I want to spare those who follow in my footsteps part of the grind and—part of the cost" (F/Abr, 1965, p. 24). Easter 1908 was also the time of the meeting in Salzburg, where Freud presented the case of the Rat Man, in speaking for five hours without interruption, moved by the desire to convey what preoccupied him. He had, as he wrote in another context to Abraham, "to recuperate from psycho-analysis by working, otherwise I should not be able to stand it" (F/Abr, 3.7.1912), and to Ferenczi: "I was depressed the whole time and anesthetized myself with writing—writing—writing" (F/Fer, 2.1.1912).

This state of mind has its origin in the affective mobilization of the analyst (cf. F/Ju, 9.3.1909), driving Freud to grasp the importance of the analyst's feelings. On 26 December 1908 he wrote to Abraham that "it has often been my experience that just those cases in which I took an excessive personal interest failed, perhaps just because of the intensity of feeling" (F/Abr, 26.12.1908). Abraham, for his part, reported to Freud that beautiful observation that he often cast a quick glance at the picture of his parents while waiting

---

[3] See also the similar statement in *Delusions and Dreams in Jensen's Gradiva* (1907a [1906], p. 90). "Eitingon quotes Freud as saying that the secret of therapy is to cure through love, and that with greatest personal effort one could perhaps overcome more difficulties in treatment but one would "lose his skin by doing so" (Ruitenbeek, 1973, p. 445).

[4] A terminological remark: in Freud's Vienna and in his intellectual milieu, the term "technique" evoked rather the "technique" of arts, that of the pianist or the painter, than that of "technology" as we understand it today. Let us not forget that in Freud's time the first of Hippocrates' aphorisms: "*Ho bios brakhus, hê de tekhnê makra*" [in Latin: "*ars longa, vita brevis*"] was quite common, especially among students of medicine, and that in this context "*technê*" = "art". So, the technique of psychoanalysis is the art of psychoanalysis, in opposition to the theory.

for a patient's reply: "The glance is always accompanied by a certain guilt feeling: what will they think of me?" (Abr/F, 7.4.1909): the affective guilt of the analyst!

Returning to C. G. Jung and Sabina Spielrein—it was only another few months later that Jung confessed to Freud that he "devote[d] a large measure of friendship to her" (Ju/F, 4.6.1909), not daring to write openly that this meant that in reality he had become her *lover*, no doubt in the wake of feelings mobilized during the treatment. The whole problem of love is experienced and developed in a very dramatic manner in this trio of the very genuine Sabina Spielrein, an embarrassed Jung trying to justify himself, and Freud, who wants to understand and at the same time exert a sort of control. He writes to Jung on 7 June 1909:

> Such experiences, though painful, are necessary and hard to avoid. . . . I myself have never been taken in quite so badly, but I have come very close to it a number of times and had *a narrow escape*. . . . But no lasting harm is done. They help us to develop the thick skin we need to dominate "countertransference" . . .; they teach us to displace our own affects to best advantage. They are a *blessing in disguise*" [in italics and in English in original (F/Ju, 7.6.1909)]. (It is in *this* letter of 1909 that the term "countertransference" appears for the *first time*. In 1910, at the Second International Psychoanalytic Congress, Freud speaks about *Future Prospects of Psychoanalytic Therapy*, and it is in the written version of this lecture that the term appears for the first time in his publications—Freud, 1910d, pp. 144–455.)

Such a conclusion, however, is not easily reached. It is remarkable that he twice uses expressions in English in the quoted letter. It seems to me, as I mentioned already, that this reflects his difficulty in dealing with these feelings and affects. As a result of these upsetting interactions, he is inclined to let the task be made by the *analysand*. With what he called the "endopsychic" solution (which, he says, he had suggested to Sabina Spielrein—F/Ju, 18.6.1909), the patient ought to be able to transform these experiences into *another constellation*—through an intrapsychic modification of feelings mobilized in the transference and through mechanisms of introjection and working through—and thus be enriched.

Freud is inclined to resort to his model of science as a means of protection: "Remember Lassalle's fine sentence about the chemist whose test-tube had cracked: 'With a slight frown over the resistance of matter, he gets on with his work'" (F/Ju, 18.6.1909). He seems to be seeking a balance between the provoked affects and his scientific *Weltanschauung*, which might enable him to keep the analytic process on an "endopsychic" level: a love affair that ought to be able to be transformed into a matter of intellectual scrutiny and introjection.

Later, in August 1909, Freud, Ferenczi, and Jung embarked on their voyage to America, where Freud gave his famous lectures at Clark University (Worcester, Mass.). Evidently, the problems that he had sought to clarify for years still occupied him, and they were the subject of intense exchanges during that voyage. They analysed each other's dreams (Jung, 1961) and tried to deepen their understanding of the unknown, shadowy, unconscious realms of the psyche. On the other hand, it is exactly in these lectures, that Freud again resorted to a scientific metaphor:

> symptoms, to take an analogy from chemistry, are precipitates of earlier experiences in the sphere of love . . ., and it is only in the raised temperature of his experience of the transference that they can be resolved and reduced to other psychical products. In this reaction the physician, if I may borrow an apt phrase from Ferenczi (1909),[5] plays the part of a catalytic ferment, which temporarily attracts to itself the affects liberated in the process. (Freud, 1910a [1909], p. 51)

Simultaneously, however, and probably under the influence of Ferenczi, Freud's and Jung's (who had written his doctoral thesis on the subject) interest in occult phenomena was again aroused. Their voyage ended with a trip to Berlin, where Ferenczi, and possibly also Freud, looking for a better understanding of "*Gedanken-Übertragung*" ["thought-transference"], met the soothsayer Frau Seidler. Ferenczi, moved by his characteristic enthusiasm, searched for soothsayers and fortune-tellers all over Europe, with Freud taking an active interest and remarking to Abraham that his daughter Anna possessed "telepathic sensitivity" (F/Abr, 9.7.1925). And let us not forget that at the famous meeting of the Committee in

---

[5] This fifth lecture in particular had been prepared by Freud with the help of Ferenczi and used his "thoughts and even some of [his] formulas" (F/Fer, 8.2.1910).

the Harz Mountains in 1921 he read a memorandum on "Psycho-Analysis and Telepathy" to his innermost circle only (published only posthumously—Freud, 1941d [1921]). A mystery also surrounds his 1922 text on the subject, published in *Imago* (Freud, 1922a): it should have been read before the Vienna Psychoanalytic Society, but for unknown reasons Freud withdrew. The text, which was already in print, nevertheless appeared (cf. p. 196). They tried in a joint effort to ferret out the secrets of *two intertwined* mysterious, embarrassing and *forbidden terrains*: firstly, that of occult communication in general; secondly, how and perhaps why love and other affects are aroused and how they are communicated in part unconsciously in transference and countertransference. How disturbing this was can be guessed from Freud's remark to Jung that a paper on countertransference seemed to be "sorely needed", adding: "of course we could not publish it, we should have to circulate copies among ourselves" (F/Ju, 31.12.1911). The previous year Freud had already remarked to Ferenczi, concerning the occult: "I would ask you to keep your thoughts to yourself for another two years and to reveal them only in 1913, but then in the *Jahrbuch*[6] and quite openly" (F/Fer, 3.12.1910). Will that be a basic secret that will suddenly reveal itself, like the discovery of the work of unconscious forces and of the Oedipus complex—and, in the end, would it destroy Freud's artfully constructed theoretical edifice with one blow?[7]

As far as Sabina Spielrein and Jung are concerned, I do not want to go into the details of what followed, especially between Sabina's mother and Jung. But let me state that it seems impossible to read Sabina's letters without being touched. Sabina Spielrein, like Emma, Jung's wife, and Gizella, Ferenczi's wife, are women of astonishing sensitivity and of great authenticity. Let us turn

---

[6] The official periodical of the International Psycho-Analytical Association at this time.

[7] Ferenczi was to attribute Jung's dissension to the fact that the "few 'occult' things [Jung] has seen sufficed to tear down the whole structure . . . of his psychoanalytical knowledge" (Fer/F, 12.5.1913), and Freud himself was to show this fear again in his reaction to Rank's notion of the birth trauma: "I have not yet overcome", Freud wrote to Ferenczi, "the first shock . . . that our sophisticated etiological edifice should be replaced by the bleak trauma of birth" (F/Fer, 26.3.1924) . . .

instead to Freud, who, on 12 October 1911, reported to Jung, that Fräulein Spielrein "turned up unexpectedly" (F/Ju, 12.10.1911). One act of the drama was over; the scene changed, and it was the start of Freud's relationship with Spielrein and the beginning of the end of Jung's. Freud, referring to a meeting of the Viennese Society, considers "Spielrein . . . very intelligent and methodical" (F/Ju, 12.11.1911), and, a few days later: "The little girl . . . is rather nice and I am beginning to understand" (F/Ju, 30.11.1911). . . .

However this may be, Freud was profoundly affected by what happened to the man whom he considered his "heir" and public representative; the theme of love, and of affects in general, in psychoanalysis did not cease to preoccupy him—all the more in that someone as close to him as Sándor Ferenczi was about to implicate him, in another manner, in a not dissimilar situation.

. . . with Ferenczi . . .

On 14 July 1911, Sándor Ferenczi wrote to Freud that he had taken into analysis Elma Pálos, the daughter of his mistress, Gizella Pálos,[8] who suffered from depression following the suicide of one of her suitors. In the course of the analysis Ferenczi fell in love with Elma, who entered "victoriously into [his] heart" (Fer/F, 3.12.11). "I could not maintain the cold superiority of the analyst with Elma", he confessed (3.12.11), and, at the end of that year, even mentioned the possibility of marriage.

So Ferenczi found himself in a veritable triangle between his mistress and her young daughter, his patient, and, even worse, tormented by doubts and a desire to know whether it was a matter of "marriage or treatment of the sickness" (Fer/F, 1.1.1912). In that same letter Ferenczi most urgently requested that Freud should take over the analysis of the young woman who had become his fiancée. "Since you request neither my inclinations nor my predic-

---

[8] Ferenczi had fallen in love with Gizella Pálos (1863–1949), born Altschul, around 1904, and had "treated" her "analytically"—probably *during* their friendly relations (Fer/F, 30.10.1909).

tions", Freud answered, "but you *require* me to take her into analysis, I am obliged to do so" (F/Fer, 2.1.1912; emphasis in original). There followed a period of insecurity, of changes of decisions, although Ferenczi was aware that in rushing headlong into the affair he set the stage for an "adventure that... has brought me close to realizing my 'family romance'". Finally, he became a "modest man" (Fer/F, 3.1.1912).

There was, in the Freud/Ferenczi correspondence of this time, an exchange of the utmost intimacy between them, with Freud revealing quite openly the most personal details of what he had learned from his analysand, Elma. Ferenczi gradually tried to distance himself of what he called a "mishap" in a letter to Freud (Fer/F, 20.1.1912). Elma, having completed a "piece of analysis" with Freud between the New Year and Easter 1912, went back to Ferenczi for finishing her analysis. In understandably very difficult circumstances, Ferenczi had to admit that he had made a mistake. In a painful to and fro he separated from Elma, encouraged to do so by Freud. There remained in him a sadness to which he did not find it easy to resign himself and perhaps never entirely accomplished it.[9]

* * *

So far, I have stressed Freud's attribution of the affects, in particular love, in the psychoanalytic encounter to the past of the other. On a close look, however, we find that his involvement made him take another seminal step. Still uncertain, we see him torn between his reservations as to the effects of an analysis on intimate relationships, being "concerned at linking the fate of our friendship with something else different and indefinable" (F/Fer, 21.4.1912), but also a deep sympathy for Ferenczi and for his and Gizella Pálos's

---

[9] It was in 1919, several years after Elma's short-lived marriage to an American named Laurvik, that Gizella and Sándor Ferenczi married. As already described in chapter two, it was on their way to the registry office that they learned that Gizella's ex-husband, Géza, had died. In "Psycho-Analysis and Telepathy" (1941d [1921], p. 191–192) Freud describes a very similar triangular relationship, in which there is also a girl who is "driven" to an analysis because a man cannot decide between her and the mother.

fate. When Ferenczi asked to be analysed by him, Freud indeed mentioned "the danger of personal alienation caused by analysis" (F/Fer, 4.5.1913), seeing the dangers more clearly than did Ferenczi; nevertheless, he analysed Elma and Ferenczi and, interestingly, even his daughter Anna twice (cf. e.g. Young-Bruehl, 1988, pp. 80–90, 103–109, 114–116, 122–125).

In effect, Freud's position was based on two theses. Firstly, it was undeniable for him that affectivity in analysis is fundamental. Freud maintained that the attempt to work with transferred emotions fails, "for when all is said and done, it is impossible to destroy anyone *in absentia* or *in effigie*" (Freud, 1912b, p. 108; cf. also 1914g, p. 152), and, in 1920, he used the metaphor of "*the dragons of primaeval days*" (1937c; emphasis added). Thus, when Ferenczi (and Otto Rank) later stressed the importance of *experience* in the analytic treatment, with Ferenczi stating that, although the aim of the cure remains in "substituting recollection for acting out", "you must catch the hare before you can cook him" (1931 [292], pp. 131–132; emphasis added), they picked up and further developed a line already opened by Freud himself.

Secondly, Freud had a somewhat protective attitude for the analyst: let us remember, for instance, his famous simile of the "surgeon, who puts aside all his feelings, even his human sympathy" (1912e, p. 115), justifying this attitude also with the fact that "this emotional coldness . . . creates . . . for the doctor a desirable *protection* for his own emotional life" (p. 115; emphasis added). He complained (F/Pf, 5.6.1910) about the "cross" of transference and the "unyielding stubbornness of the illness" (5.6.1910). Freud talked about the analyst's cross, whose integrity and identity is threatened by regression and being flooded by sexuality and psychosis. The analyst could bear the cross when the patient was "kept in sexual abstinence, in unrequited love", although this, as Freud adds, "of course is not always possible" (5.6.1910). And Freud concludes: "The more you let him find love the sooner you will get his complexes, but the smaller is the final success, as he gives up the fulfilments of the complexes only because he can exchange them for the results of the transference" (5.6.1910).

Freud's conclusion was that it is absolutely *vital* to "surmount countertransference" (F/Ju, 2.2.1910), and not only that, but to do so *"completely"* (Nunberg & Federn, 1962, 9.3.1910). (Binswanger also recalled Freud's statement that in every analysis countertransference must first be "recognized" and then "surmounted", and that only then one can be "free"—F/Bins, 20.2.1913.)

On the other hand, however, Freud uses a well-known metaphor in describing how important the unconscious of the analyst is as "a receptive organ" capturing the messages coming from the patient—the "telephone receiver . . . adjusted to the transmitting microphone" (1912e), a device that enables the doctor's unconscious "to reconstruct that unconscious, which has determined the patient's free associations" (1912e). (It is interesting that for this *positive* aspect of the functioning of the analyst's mind he does not use the term countertransference in opposition to the later post-Freudian use of the word.) In *Totem and Taboo* (Freud, 1912–13) he postulates a transmission of "psychic processes. . . . For psychoanalysis has shown us that everyone possesses in his unconscious mental activity an apparatus which enables him to . . . undo the distortions which in other people have imposed on the expression of their feelings" (Freud, 1912–13, p. 159)—an idea that Ferenczi immediately described as "new and excellent" (Fer/F, 23.6.1913). Or, picking up Ferenczi's idea of "the dialogues between the unconsciouses" (Ferenczi, 1915 [159], p. 109), Freud states that "the *Ucs.* of one human being can react upon that of another" (Freud, 1915e, p. 194).

It seems that Freud continued to stay in what we could call a "dialectic" position—on the one side the exigency to *overcome* transference and countertransference, and on the other the fundamental *need* for transference as the fundamental motivation of the cure and for countertransference as the basic tool of understanding.

For Ferenczi, who had the experience of both roles—those of analyst and analysand—the problem was even more painful. Driven by his own conflicts, he was nevertheless able to develop a view of the therapeutic relationship that proved to be very fruitful, notwithstanding the sometimes extreme form in which he presented it. These events very probably contributed to his increasing understanding that the analyst's attitude was a *variable* in the therapeutic equation and that, for that reason, he put it at the centre of his interests. It was distressing for him, in fact, in that network of relationships between Freud, Elma and himself, not to be able to distinguish *"transference"* from *"real"* feelings. He must have suffered in distinguishing between the roles of analyst, analysand, lover, friend, and follower when he threw himself wholly into those relationships. It is indeed understandable that he was able to see with great acuity how patients might sometimes suffer from what he felt was a "hypocrisy" (Ferenczi, 1933 [294], pp. 158–159) of the analyst's total "abstinence"—that is, in hiding himself behind an attitude of reserve and distance for defensive reasons and protection. (He must have felt that Freud's attitude towards him, during their analysis, was too distant: "He was too great for me, too much of the father . . ."—Fer/Grod, 1982, pp. 36–37. If today we have a much more differentiated view of "abstinence", this is also part of Ferenczi's legacy.)

Freud, for his part, reached a sort of conclusion: since, firstly, a method working with present feelings also "implies conjuring up a piece of real life; and for that reason it cannot always be harmless and unobjectionable" (Freud, 1914g, p. 152), and since, secondly, "healing through love" is something that is *sought* by *the analysand*, but which must fail in the end because of the "patient's incapacity for love" (Freud, 1914c, p. 101), he concludes: "In my opinion, therefore, it is *not permissible* to disavow the indifference one has developed by keeping the counter-transference in check" (Freud, 1915a [1914], p. 164; translated for this edition, emphasis added).

Freud was preoccupied not only by affects of sexualized love, recognizing already in 1905 that in analysis also *hostile* tendencies are regularly aroused (1905e [1901], 117), and regarding as the turning point in the "Rat Man"-case his vigorous and consistent interpretation of *negative* transference (cf. Freud, 1909d, pp. 199–200, 209; and 1955a [1907–08], p. 281). In 1937, writing about the professional hazards of psychoanalysis, he came near to a broader idea of negative influence coming from the analysands: "We are driven into drawing a disagreeable analogy with the effect of X-rays on people who handle them without taking special precautions" (Freud, 1937c, 249).

After the Budapest Congress (1918) —
Ferenczi's contributions

At the Budapest Congress (1918) Freud referred to the necessity of diversifying the analytic technique, particularly in pronouncing that it "grew up in the treatment of hysteria", but that "the phobias have already made it necessary for us to go beyond our former limits" (Freud, 1919a [1918], p. 165; cf. also Freud, 1912e, p. 111). Already in 1912 he had implored Ferenczi to work in this area (F/Fer, 28.1.1912) and was pleased about Ferenczi's growing cooperation with Rank (F/Fer, 24.8.1922; unpublished letter to Rank, 8.9.1922).

After the Budapest Congress, Freud seems to have preferred to leave the largely unresolved question of the practical impact of affective forces more and more to his circle, in the first place to Ferenczi and to Rank, expecting new ideas from them, offering encouragement in the form, among others, of a prize for the best study on the correlation of theory and technique (Freud, 1922d). Apparently, his hopes were high that this problem could be solved by his closest collaborators.

There is a clear connection between this and Ferenczi's radicalization of the concept of transference in 1926, when he, following Rank, regards "the relation of patient to analyst as the cardinal point of the analytic material and . . . *every* dream, *every* gesture, *every* parapraxis, *every* aggravation or improvement in the condition of the patient as above all an expression of transference and resistance" (Ferenczi, 1926 [271], p. 225).

This is also the period when Ferenczi turns to another analyst–colleague: Georg Groddeck. Groddeck was to become a close partner for the exchange of ideas and even a partner in a mutual analysis. It is in this interaction between Ferenczi and Rank and between Ferenczi and Groddeck, and under the influence of both, that Ferenczi's last works were created—those works that give him his place in the history of ideas in psychoanalysis. Practically the whole psychoanalytic community has taken up the central role of analysing the transference, the importance—beyond the oedipal bond—of the mother, and, to some extent, of traumatism; forgetting that historically this is the legacy of Ferenczi, who developed these ideas more or less close to Freud. The latter, incidentally, acknowledged their importance a couple of times (he states that he values "the joint book [by Ferenczi and Rank] as a corrective of my view of the role of repetition or acting out in analysis"—circular letter to the Committee, 15.2.1924; Freud & Abraham, 1965, p. 345). Ferenczi's research boils down to a field concept of *interactions*—in the end, one of intersubjectivity (without ever using this term, as far as we know)—yet avoiding a "cheap" interactionism. Experimenting with changing roles of the analyst (active therapy and relaxation), becoming aware of how important the analyst's attitude is for the analytic cure, and also breaking a taboo by taking into consideration his own feelings and his inner reaction, he finally and logically comes to centre his interest on countertransference and on the metapsychology of the analyst, calling "for the creation of a special hygiene for the analyst" (1928 [283], p. 98). His tendency to experiment led him still farther, and he even tried out "mutual analysis" with some analysands (Ferenczi, 1985 [1932]). He would probably have liked to do it also with Freud—when Freud's cancer had been diagnosed, Ferenczi offered to analyse him. Freud turned the offer down, choosing instead somatic therapy—for example, the so-called Steinach-operation (Jones, 1957, p. 104).

The topics of deep regressive states, of the repetition of trauma in the analytic interaction, of the central role of countertransference and, consequently, of the necessity of a metapsychology of the analyst, became a subject of controversies between Sándor Ferenczi and Sigmund Freud, particularly after 1927, until Ferenczi's death in 1933. These controversies acted, as Balint reminds us, as a trauma for the analytic community, and became for long years taboo topics, surrounded by silence, all the more in that Jones's Freud biography had treated this subject very insufficiently. (Ferenczi's heir, Michael Balint, writes in a draft for an introduction to Ferenczi's *Clinical Diary* that "the aftermath of Jones' Biography was a spate of acrimonious publications"—Draft Introduction, in Ferenczi, 1985 [1932], p. 220). Ferenczi himself (and also Otto Rank, a friend of his for some time), though not deleted from the historical record of psychoanalysis, were viewed as being disturbed, even mentally ill (Jones, 1957, p. 47), and their theories were considered an outcome of this supposed mental illness.

This second, "unaccepted" part of the heritage was, however, brought to London by Michael Balint, and there it fell on fertile ground in the British "Middle Group"; it has since, through their influence—that of Paula Heimann, Margaret Little, Donald Winnicott, and others—infiltrated present psychoanalytic thinking. Anna Freud, too, expressed her admiration for Ferenczi several times (cf., e.g., her letter to M. Balint dated 23.5.1935 [Balint Archives]), and she borrowed one of her central terms, "developmental lines", from him. The American interpersonal school is also in a direct line with his thinking, mainly through the mediation of Clara Thompson, who had gone to Europe for analysis with Ferenczi and had subsequently analysed Harry Stack Sullivan. In addition, some of these issues re-emerge in "self psychology" (the concept of empathy—P. Ornstein worked closely with Michael Balint before becoming an associate of Heinz Kohut's; John Gedo, an early associate of Kohut, made a thorough study of Ferenczi). Whether we are aware of it or not, Ferenczi's legacy is still with us.

CHAPTER SEVEN

The Correspondence

A correspondence is a sensitive object indeed. Born in intimacy, it suddenly finds itself exposed to the full light of day, as if a psychoanalytic session, a scene between husband and wife, or a moment between lovers were abruptly stripped of its veils and paraded in public for all to see. The historian justifies his action on the grounds of the usefulness of the knowledge thus gained, and likewise the historian of psychoanalysis before his own professional community.

Now the historians of psychoanalysis are often "suspect" in the eyes of the practitioner, who vaguely feels that the historical approach goes hand in hand with a distancing from the ideas and ideals that govern contemporary practice—sometimes including that of the historian himself—and calls, like it or no, for an assimilation of conceptions rediscovered in the bygone days of our science, of viewpoints set aside, consigned to oblivion, and on occasion deprecated—notions that pose a number of inconvenient questions. Even if these researches lead to the discovery of forgotten meeting points and the reasons for certain choices, the weight of the past and its whys and wherefores—the curiosity of sons and daughters subjecting their parents' lives to scrutiny—must inevitably arouse anxieties: what if this past were not as ideal as we would wish it to have been handed down or to imagine it?

In the letters at issue here, our curiosity initially uncovers detail after detail of the everyday lives and peculiarities of the two correspondents, including foibles and "human" aspects that they share with each other and ourselves, all embedded in the dynamics of the transference and their common enthusiasm for the discovery of human beings in their innermost recesses. We read in higgledy-piggledy juxtaposition of the reality problems of the day—the war, food shortages, Ferenczi's military service, the fate of Freud's children, Ferenczi's premarital and marital history with Gizella, and a variety of comments about the analytic community and its organizations. When Freud writes "I . . . am very much inclined toward plagiarism" (8 February 1910), and when indiscretions abound on patients—for instance, Jones's companion Loé Kann, who was in analysis with Freud from 1912 until 1914, while Ferenczi, for his part, had Ernest in analysis (in 1913), or Elma Pálos—we encounter a different person from the Freud of the published "official" writings, even if certain traits overlap with those already familiar to us, such as his enthusiasm at the beginning of the Great War (23 August 1914): "The rush of enthusiasm . . . swept me along with it." Elsewhere, he says bluntly: "Spielrein crazy [meschugge, Yiddish for crazy], writes that I have something against her" (16 May 1914).

With outspoken candour, he criticizes Groddeck (22 June 1917), describes Tausk as "intractably meschugge" (19 January 1918), and admits that he cannot muster any "real sympathy" for Tausk even after his death (10 July 1919). After referring to his pupils Rank and Sachs, he suddenly declares: "As I see it, I am still the giant" (27 December 1917). Many more examples could be adduced.

Freud expressed the idea several times that patients were good for providing "us with a livelihood" (Ferenczi, 1988 [1932], note of May 1932, p. 93), and, for instance, that he felt like a machine for earning money (F/Fer, 13.2.1910, p. 138). In 1920 (on 26 November) we find him complaining that he had to work for six hours in English; later, he confessed that he would give up working if he had more money. By then, he was 71 years of age (22 April 1928)!

We also see him delving in depth with Ferenczi into certain aspects of their common research, including occultism, sometimes rather like two schoolboys, and on other occasions in the form of a collaboration between a genius and an extraordinary man that was directed toward a deepening, along quite unusual pathways, of psychoanalysis, the problems of the transference and of human relations in general, with an "urge towards de-occultization [*Drang nach Desokkultierung*]" (Fer/F, 24 July 1915). Freud counselled Ferenczi against publishing anything about this lest such an act have the effect of "a bomb" (20 March 1925).

As for Sándor Ferenczi, we witness the speed of his attachment to Freud: in 1914, when—for the first time since 1908—they were unable to spend their vacation together, Ferenczi succumbed to depression (20 July 1914). At the same time Freud reproached him: "You grasp things differently and for that reason often put a strain on me" (22 July 1914). However, he also told his Budapest friend that in December 1914 he had "exactly two patients, both Hungarian!" (2 December 1914); and on another occasion, he openly averred that he would have liked Ferenczi to marry Mathilde (2 March 1917).

Ferenczi was from the outset very alive to the analyst's involvement in the analytic process. Already in 1909 he reported that he dreamed a great deal, that he understood himself better, and that his analytic activity, too, was now more satisfying (26 October 1909).

In 1916 he wrote: "I am incredibly much indebted to the last analysis for my analytic technique." He seems to have understood the profound significance of "*repetition* in the treatment" (28 July 1916; emphasis in original).

Stressing the maternal role of the analyst, Ferenczi mentioned the therapeutic clumsiness of the Berliners and in particular of Abraham (1 September 1924), whom he described as driven by "ambition and jealousy" (18 March 1924). His antipathy—or reserve—toward the latter was manifestly intensified by the tensions between his doctor and friend Georg Groddeck and Karl Abraham. Ferenczi favoured a technique devoid of excesses (20 December 1927) and wrote on 10 January 1929 of his pleasure at having found a style of working that enabled him "to work calmly and successfully".

Freud and Ferenczi were both conscious of the incompleteness of Ferenczi's periods of analysis; Freud even referred to an

"Analysenversuch" ["attempt at analysis"], which he described as "finished, not terminated" (16 November 1916). Ferenczi was consequently very impressed by the therapeutic efficacy of short treatments. He even wondered (3 November 1917) why his patients stayed in analysis with him for more than a year: "There is some error in this!"

This written record throws light on Ferenczi's career and development. He had joined the union of social-democratic physicians, as he wrote to Freud on 24 November 1918. At the same time, 180 signatures had been collected for his professorial appointment (25 October 1918). There would be 1,000 for another petition (24 November 1918; cf. also Erös & Giampieri, 1987). In 1918 Ferenczi foresaw the future of Hungary—the coming of "a clerical-reactionary tide . . . [which] will harm the young Hungarian psychoanalysis" (26 December 1918). Not long afterward, he wrote (28 August 1919): "After the unbearable 'Red terror,' which lay heavy on one's spirit like a nightmare, we now have the White one." Later still, on 3 September 1923, Ferenczi was to express some satisfaction at the improvement of political conditions in Hungary.

At the beginning of the 1920s, the correspondence hints at what was tantamount to a Freud–Rank–Ferenczi triangle: Freud was pleased at the greater intimacy between Rank and Ferenczi (24 August 1922) but presently informed Ferenczi that he was unable to put him up because Rank had taken his room (Christmas 1922). Moreover, Freud suddenly showed himself to be jealous of Rank, telling Ferenczi off for corresponding with him and not enough with himself (20 March 1924), at a time when he still saw Rank as his successor (26 March 1924). So it was that Freud was able to write of Rank on 1 June 1923 that "his finding is great indeed", but a year later, on 29 August 1924, that Rank would not have written his book on the trauma of birth had he been analysed. The process of separation between Rank and Freud was as distressing as a messy divorce, and between the two stood Ferenczi, unswerving in his loyalty to Freud but suffering nonetheless from their split. It is impossible to overemphasize the sadness of a separation between an old man afraid of being abandoned and a younger man who felt that he was not understood (18 September 1931); the dilemma between *"entfernen"* [distancing] and *"entfremden"* [alienation] arose, and, as so often in human relations, could not be resolved in terms of binary logic but underwent oscillations, pain, and a test of the firmness of the bonds that united the two men, notwithstanding all their difficulties.

The correspondence also enlightens us about the Gizella/Elma affair. It was on 14 July 1911 that Ferenczi informed Freud that he had decided to take into analysis Elma, the daughter of his mistress Gizella (who was at the time married to Géza Pálos). He wrote in October that the analysis was going well, and then one of her suitors killed himself for her. . . . Matters were becoming more complicated, and Ferenczi explained to Freud that his relationship with her could no longer be seen as merely benevolent or paternal: "To all appearances, she has won my heart" (3 December 1911). He insisted that Freud take her into analysis; Freud replied on 2 January 1912 that, since he was not asking him for his opinion and preferences but seemed to be making a demand, he ultimately felt compelled to accede.

Elma's analysis thus began on this note, with many indiscretions between the two men and back-and-forth swings in Ferenczi's position: now he wanted to marry her, now to have her back in analysis in Budapest—as a condition for a possible marriage—once she had finished her period of analysis with Freud in Vienna at Easter. This whole confused situation was indeed proof, if proof be needed, of Freud's contention (1915a [1914], p. 168) that transference love is genuine love (cf. Section 2). Yes, Ferenczi did abandon his position as a psychoanalyst and create a triangle between Gizella, his then mistress and future wife, and her daughter, Elma, his analysand, later Freud's analysand, and afterwards again his own analysand, thus providing grist for the mill of anyone who considers Ferenczi's later positions to be too audacious, for this was admittedly a problematic episode in his professional and private life. Again, as we know, he suffered for many years the personal consequences of this affair in the form of depression and hypochondria and had great difficulty in recovering his inner equilibrium. The episode is characteristic of Ferenczi's temperament and his tendency to involve himself unstintingly in the therapeutic situation, and perhaps also of his disinclination to undertake a (protective and defensive) split between his professional and private lives. It was not the analyst alone but the *whole man* who engaged in these relationships, setting out with remarkable courage on a voyage of discovery.

Nor did the episode with Elma—the "Elma affair"—help Ferenczi to become Freud's "equal", as the latter desired, even if this demand was not unambiguous: "I would have wished for you to tear yourself away from the infantile role and take your place next to me as a companion with equal rights, which you did not succeed in doing" (2 October 1910). The fact that Freud was Elma's analyst did not make the relationship between the two men any easier. As it happens, Freud corresponded with Gizella about this behind Ferenczi's back (for instance: "My last letter to you was meant for you only; it was too straightforward for him" [11 February 1917]); Gizella, of course, showed Ferenczi these missives. However, Ferenczi, too, asked Freud to tell Gizella certain things on his behalf, as in his letter of 24 March 1917. He also wrote, as it happens in the condensed form of a single sentence: "I have already gone through this period, in which you analyzed Elma and I subsequently couldn't marry her" (12 March 1913).

Psychoanalysis: passion and concern

"Since 1909 we have covered a nice piece of trail with each other, always hand in hand, and it won't be any different for the short stretch that still remains to be tread" (F/Fer, 25 October 1927; translator's note: *sic*). "Your enclosed paper . . . testifies to that superior maturity that you have acquired in the last few years and in which no one approaches you" (F/Fer, 4 January 1928).

Freud was concerned above all with identifying the *temptations* operating *against* analysis:

> My recommendations on technique which I gave back then were essentially negative. I considered the most important thing to emphasize what one should not do to, to demonstrate the temptations that work against analysis. Almost everything that is positive that one should do I left to "tact", which has been introduced by you. But what I achieved in so doing was

that the obedient ones didn't take notice of the elasticity of these dissuasions and subjected themselves to them as if they were taboos. That had to be revised at some time, without, of course, revoking the obligations. (F/Fer, 4 January 1928)

Freud manifestly had some misgivings in this discussion about tact: "All those who have no tact will see in this a justification of arbitrariness, i.e., of the subjective factor, i.e., of the influence of one's own unrestrained complexes" (4 January 1928). He was afraid that this notion might allow "subjectivity" to indulge in excesses, which would run counter to his ideal of an objective science. As it happens, he provided his own answer: "What we undertake in reality is a weighing-out, which remains mostly pre-conscious, of the various reactions" (4 January 1928). Ferenczi's exploration may have shown how this subjectivity is mobilized and what the analyst can do with it (4 January 1928).

In his letter of 13 December 1931, Freud raised the question of gratifications, and in particular the degree of *erotic gratifications* in the treatment. In our view, his allusions to Ferenczi's tendency to eroticize the relationship involved material with which he must have been familiar through the two men's intimate friendship and Ferenczi's total, unreserved openness toward him, as well as what he may have known through his analysis; and the turmoil over Elma must also have played a part. After all, Ferenczi tended to allow himself to get involved in relationships, but now he was doing so in the full knowledge and consciousness of his actions, while at the same time endeavouring to understand and interpret. In other words, he tried to proceed to the very *limit* of possible engagement and subsequently, through interpretation, to initiate the process of disengagement. Freud, who was much more aloof, manifestly did not appreciate this. The censorship displayed by Jones in his biography of Freud (1955) clearly shows the extent to which the *pupils* around Freud and Ferenczi played a part by poisoning the atmosphere with their own anxieties. Ferenczi understood perfectly well what was at stake. He wrote on 27 December 1931 that he wished to publish his results because he thought that such a decision should be taken after *"Einsicht des Autors"* [according to the author's judgement]. It was, he said, an oversimplification to describe him as a second Stekel. He intimated to Freud that he was very hurt by the tone of his previous letter, that he hoped that their relationship would not be called into question by his scientific development, and that, if this were to happen, it would quickly be restored.

Much has been made, too, of the fact that Freud wanted to bring Ferenczi back to the fold by conferring upon him the responsibilities of the presidency of the IPA. Freud might admittedly have liked Ferenczi to renew his identification, by this office, with the aims of the IPA, but perhaps he also wanted him not to lose himself—as Freud feared—in his research. Isolated in Budapest, Ferenczi said that he was more interested in psychoanalytic technique than in its politics (6 November 1929; 5 January 1930). Later, he again adopted a clear-cut position in his letter of 1 May 1932, to the effect that he wished to give free rein to his inner researches, and he asked Freud: "You want to have a president whose interest is in part manacled in this way?" Freud made it clear on 12 May 1932 that he did not want Ferenczi to remain in isolation, and that he thought the presidency might be a kind of forcible therapy[1] ["*Gewaltkur*"]. This led on to the famous passage in which he urged Ferenczi to leave the island of dreams he inhabited with his fantasy-children and mix with the struggle of men. Ferenczi replied resolutely on 19 May that he was unfortunately unable to agree to forcible therapy for a disease that he could not recognize as such, but that he would, in a different context, have considered it a favour to be charged with the presidency of the Association, having contributed to its foundation.

His little notes—such as one dated 22 May 1932, stating that in his opinion castration and penis envy did not play such a large part in female sexuality as had been attributed to them, and adding: "What has been your experience?"—went unanswered.

Organizational problems and the arrival of a new generation were also casting a shadow: the name of Hartmann appears in Freud's letter of 13 June 1932 as one of the new editors of the *Internationale Zeitschrift*, and those of Kris and Waelder for *Imago*. Freud showed himself to be very irritated by Fenichel's espousal of Reich's "Bolshevism" . . . *Tempora mutantur*—as we can see.

---

[1] [*Translator's note*: The published translation, "drastic measure", fails to convey the sense of the original.]

The correspondence exchanged in the autumn of 1932 shows that the affective relationship between the two men had been further exacerbated by a "confusion of tongues. . . ." Ferenczi remarked: "You certainly know just as well as I do what a loss it means for both of us that my visit with you could transpire in such a way" (27 September 1932). Ferenczi was referring to his visit to Freud at the time of his journey to Baden, where, in the presence of a "witness" (who was none other than Brill), he says, he was received very coolly. Freud had taken leave of him without even shaking his hand. To Ferenczi's remark, Freud replied: "Objectively, I think I would be in a position to point out to you the theoretical error in your construction, but what for?" (2 October 1932)—hardly a very respectful way of countering one's interlocutor's argument! Be that as it may, Freud confirmed that the two men had "an intimate community of life, feeling, and interest" (11 January 1933), and ended "Always yours." Contrary to rumour and legend, this correspondence shows that, even if their relationship had deteriorated, a bond, and a moving one at that, persisted between the two men. Ferenczi subsequently—on 29 March 1933— begged Freud to go to a safe country, for example the United Kingdom, saying that he himself thought he might go to Switzerland if the political situation worsened. Freud answered: "The discussions between us . . . can wait, and will only profit from lying fallow" (2 April 1933), while declaring his intention not to leave Vienna for the time being. He also informed Ferenczi, as early as 1933, that the German Jews could no longer leave Germany—a historical fact that is easily forgotten! Ferenczi wrote on 9 April to say that he was quite happy to leave the discussion in abeyance.

In his last letter, Ferenczi was still conveying birthday greetings to Freud: "The date of your birthday is still in our memory" (4 May 1933). Gizella added: "I don't know what I can believe and hope" (4 May 1933). The end was indeed at hand, for Ferenczi died on 22 May 1933.

CHAPTER EIGHT

Ferenczi—dissident

"Dissidence" is defined in the *Oxford Dictionary* as "disagreeing, esp. with an established government, system etc." Obviously it is an expression from the vocabulary of political or religious totalitarian movements, which consider it necessary, for their reaction to be effective, that people must be loyal to, and have solidarity with, all the details of a political programme. In what follows I should like to try to define generally the historical factors—personal, institutional, and intellectual—connected with this problem, and in particular the case of Ferenczi.

"To dissent" seems to be something other than "dissidence". The latter refers to a group process and has political and institutional connotations that are ecclesiastical or religious in origin. It also refers more to external action, while "dissent" has, rather, to do with internal feelings.

In order to investigate this question, we may take a quick look at the circumstances that led to the psychoanalytical *movement*, that movement which was to serve the "cause" ["*die Sache*"—Freud]. Freud's vain hope of being able to take over the territory of psychiatry as a "conquistador" with Jung led Binswanger to say that

Freud had lost the scientific heritage for the second or third time (Bins/F, 4.5.1926). After Freud's disappointment when he found no attachment to psychiatry by Bleuler and Jung—as he had hoped— he hit upon the idea that the psychoanalysts could affiliate with the International Fraternity of Ethics and Culture founded by the Swiss apothecary, Alfred Knapp (F/Ju, 13.1.1910). Obviously he was originally uncertain which form of union would be the most favourable; it was not until New Year's Day 1910 that he cautiously asked Ferenczi concerning a form of association for *psychoanalysts*. Ferenczi replied on 2 January 1910, by return of post, and with his characteristic enthusiasm: "I think your suggestion . . . is a very useful one", and he immediately urged a strict choice of candidates. In conversation with Ferenczi, Freud finally abandoned the idea of affiliation to the International Fraternity (F/Fer, 13.2.1910) and instructed Ferenczi to work out the statutes in agreement with him and to propose them at the Nuremberg Congress, where the IPA was indeed founded.

A further turning-point in the history of psychoanalysis was the foundation of the "Secret Committee" around Freud, in the beginning consisting of Freud himself, Karl Abraham, Sándor Ferenczi, Ernest Jones, Otto Rank, and Hanns Sachs. Ferenczi's *original idea* was "the wish that a small group of men could be thoroughly analysed by [Freud himself] so that they could represent the pure theory unadulterated by personal complexes, and thus build an unofficial inner circle in the *Verein* and serve as centres where others (beginners) could come and learn the work" (Jo/F, 30.7.1912).

Each of the Committee's members should, in other words, undergo a purification process with the Master himself, an initiation procedure that would enable him to act as a representative of "pure" theory and "exact" technique and to initiate others. Here we have to remind ourselves of the background of Jung's impending dissension. The Committee's first task, then, was to discuss the work of the "Zürcher" critically—that is, negatively. Freud's *On the History of the Psycho-Analytical Movement* (Freud, 1914d) belongs in this context. Here Freud uses the word "movement" for the first time in relation to psychoanalysis (with one exception: in a footnote in 1907a [1906] added by him in 1912).

Now we come to the question of what Freud, against this background, would say on the problem of whether or not Ferenczi was a dissident. Incidentally, "dissidence" is not to be found in Guttman's *Freud Concordance*, but on the other hand "dissent" appears three times, and "dissensions" four times, two of them in the political sense. My hypothesis is that in his conception of dissidence the *personal* element played a great part. This is proved by the fact that he tolerated Binswanger well, because he was reasonably detached from him, and in addition Binswanger's sanatorium rendered him important services: he referred his patients for clinical treatment there. On the other hand, he wrote: "Your book has . . . also disappointed me" (F/Bins, 7.2.1923).

As far as Ferenczi is concerned, the relationship was difficult from the beginning—see "the incident at Palermo"—but very intimate. Ferenczi, however, wished for *even more intimacy* (Fer/F, 5.2.1910). This demand on Ferenczi's part was actually *never satisfied* by Freud, as appears, for example, in a letter from Freud to Ferenczi which has become famous: " . . . Since the case of Fliess, this need has been extinguished in me" (F/Fer, 6.10.1910).

Moreover, he first broke off his personal relations with Jung also, and only then did he manoeuvre to push Jung, too, out of the movement with the help of his "ring-bearers" (cf. Paskauskas, 1988). I believe that Ferenczi's example shows fairly clearly how dominant a part the personal element plays: when Ferenczi went to America, Freud felt abandoned, the relationship deteriorated, and he became cold as ice; then when Ferenczi came back and pacified him, everything went much better again. Doctrine actually played a very small part at that moment. In his definition of dissidence Freud was obviously strongly influenced by his desertion anxiety.

"Finally I should like to know when you are leaving and when you want to say goodbye. You can't go so far away without saying goodbye" (F/Fer, 6.7.1926). " . . . accept from me the obligation to give me your news often and enough" (F/Fer, 19.9.1926). "I find *you* more reserved than you were before America. That damned country!" (F/Fer, 2.8.1927).

As the analyst needs his analysands for his psychic equilibrium, so Freud obviously also needed his pupils. Besides, he clearly suffered from the "splendid isolation" of the 1890s, connected with his self-exploration; this was easier in dialogue. But this dialogue was very difficult, as witness the Fliess episode and also Ferenczi. As he himself said, love and hate mingled very easily:

> My emotional life has always insisted that I should have an intimate friend and a hated enemy. I have always been able to provide myself afresh with both, and it has not infrequently happened that the ideal situation of childhood has been so completely reproduced that friend and enemy have come together in a single individual. (Freud, 1900a, p. 483)

Perhaps he was also concerned with the *preservation* of his own thoughts, about which he spoke several times: that he had no double, no twin transference. Moreover, there is what Roustang (1976) worked out as a "*Maître–élève* relationship" between Freud and his pupils.

In this context, Freud could see other people's struggles for independence only to a very inadequate extent, and he underestimated them. In the case of Ferenczi, who reproached him with not having pointed out the "negative transference", Freud justified himself by saying that it was not there at all (Freud, 1937c). Today we can assert that it did come out quite openly in the correspondence. In the case of Rank, whom he actually "used" for a long time almost as a part of himself, it was "an almost unbelievable experience" for Freud (F/Fer, 27.8.1924) that "little" Rank suddenly became independent, even though in a "defiant" way: "For 15 years he was my blameless helper and faithful son. Now, ever since he has believed he has made a great discovery, he is behaving so mulishly that I envisage his return from America only with great anxiety" (F/AS, 11.8.1924). "Now which is the real Rank, the one I have known for 15 years, or the one whom Jones has been wanting to show me for years?" (F/Fer, 29.8.1924).

The group around Freud was a male group, and this "homosexuality", just as his theory signifies, easily turned to paranoia; *Totem and Taboo* (1912–13) seems to mirror his existential situation with his co-workers. The Fliess story and all that followed it— Adler, Stekel, Jung—is also a good illustration of that; he himself says about Adler: "Adler is a little Fliess redivivus, just as paranoid. Stekel, his appendage, is at least called Wilhelm" (F/Fer, 16.12.1910).

And Freud came to understand that he had developed his theory on paranoia from Fliess's case.

If Ferenczi did not want to become a dissident, it was because he never really wanted to break with Freud. On the contrary, he tried to get Freud to recognize him. Even though he criticized Freud in his *Clinical Diary* and expressed opinions other than his, he still remained faithful to Freud's *person* and to psychoanalysis. This was obviously dissent, but not dissidence.

Nevertheless, Ferenczi was different from Freud; his interests and his sensibility were not the same as Freud's. Why should we call this difference heresy or dissidence? He was loyal to Freud, so, as we have said, it was not dissidence. He did not reject Freud's theories, so it was not heresy; he "*took nothing away*" from the ensemble of Freud's views [haeresis from Greek: "*hairo*", take away]. As late as 1930, moreover, Freud was writing to Ferenczi: "In reality we can be satisfied that even the theoretical differences between us go no further than is inevitable with two different, independent workers, if they do not have a continuous exchange of thought and influence each other mutually!" (F/Fer, 20.1.1930). In 1924 Freud wrote to Otto Rank: "If only Ferenczi would not always set so much value on complete agreement with me! I make no such demands, in God's name, let us for once have a different point of view!" (F/R, 23.3.1924).

But he himself did not always contribute to this tolerance, especially in situations in which he allied himself with one of his co-workers against another; he wrote to Karl Abraham, referring to Jung: "You are closer to my intellectual constitution because of racial kinship" (F/Abr, 3.5.1908), while *on the same day* he wrote to Jung about Abraham: "You have every advantage over him" (F/Ju, 3.5.1908).

As far as Ferenczi is concerned, he also showed loyalty to the IPA (cf. Ferenczi, 1911 [1910]; 1928). He even went so far as to show himself to be loyal in the personal field also, in what was certainly a questionable way: when in 1926 he met Rank by chance in Pennsylvania Station in New York, he is said not even to have greeted him: "He was my best friend", said Rank, "and he refused to speak to me" (Lieberman, 1985, p. 267). Or did Ferenczi simply want to avoid a painful argument?

At the time of crisis at the end of the 1920s and the beginning of the 1930s, would Freud have said that Ferenczi was a dissident? He did in fact say that he was ill—for example, in a letter to Jones:

"... for years Ferenczi has no longer been with us, indeed, not even with himself.... Simultaneously a mental degeneration in the form of paranoia developed with uncanny consistency. Central to this was the conviction that I did not love him enough, did not want to acknowledge his work, and also that I had analysed him badly. His technical innovations were connected with this.... On this confusion his once so brilliant intelligence was extinguished. But let us keep his sad end a secret between us" [F/Jo, 29.5.1933 Original in German]

In connection with Rank, he also wrote of his "neurosis which has become manifest" (F/Fer, 4.9.1924).

Another interesting connection between therapeutic intentions for these "sick people" and for the "*Movement*" arises from the fact that Freud wanted to make Adler, Jung, Rank, and Ferenczi presidents, in order to bind them institutionally to the movement. Thus, Adler, as "the" personality of the Vienna Association, was to be bound to it in the hope that holding the office, he would also defend Freud's psychoanalysis. The same idea may have played a part in Freud's decision to make Jung—who in his first letters had already cast doubts on Freud's basic assumptions—President of the IPA. Later Freud was to try to make Otto Rank president [*Obmann*] of the Vienna Association, precisely when he began to express thoughts deviating from Freud's theory, and Ferenczi was, at Freud's request, to take over at one point the presidency of the IPA, when his friendship with Freud was put at risk because of his technical experiments. When the personal bonds became too weak, it was suddenly the "movement" that had to take over the commitment.

The Freud–Rank and Freud–Ferenczi relationships could be compared with the ending of analyses. However, these relationships were from a certain point of view mutual analyses. On the one hand, the exchange of analytical experiences, orally or through work-projects, is also an "analysis" to a certain extent; on the other hand, Freud interpreted the relationships analytically, not only in Ferenczi's case, but also with Rank and Abraham—which led

Ferenczi to say: "My hope, not unjustified as I believe, is that free discussion, analytically as well, can be possible also between well-tried friends. I must admit that I should no longer feel comfortable in the one-sided role of the analysand. Do you consider such mutual openness to be impossible?" (Fer/Freud, 14.2.1930).

The end of the relationship with Rank was also like the end of an analysis, with a "to and fro", as is often the case, in separations or other processes of giving up affectively important relationships—and with following self-assertion when the process has ended. So Rank writes to Freud: "You are obviously putting the personal relationships between you and me where they have absolutely no business to be" (R/F, 9.8.1924).

Ferenczi only half accomplished this self-assertion and detachment.

To become an original thinker also means that the whole of previous tradition—in our case, the work of Freud—is not completely taken over. In this sense an original thinker, looked at more closely, is perhaps a heretic, in that he thrusts aside the points of view of his predecessor in favour of others. We can, however, also say that Freud himself is one of those thinkers (like Wittgenstein) who must always begin anew. I refer, among others, to the turning-point around 1920, to name only one. We could also say that each of these dissidents has further developed a part of Freud's thoughts: Abraham the model of melancholia, Klein the death instinct and the second topic, Ferenczi object relations, Jung mythology and the archaic heredity, and so on.

Now if, like Freud, one has the ideal of regarding psychoanalysis as a homogeneous movement, this is not betrayal and dissidence. Dissidence exists only if we start from the point of view of a "movement". If not, it is "going one's own way" and becoming an independent thinker, at the *cost* of a process of detachment, such as Paula Heimann's towards Melanie Klein and Bion's towards Klein (he had to go off to Los Angeles in order to become an original thinker).

From the point of view of the *history of science*, we can also regard this as an change of paradigm. Ferenczi was certainly a changer of paradigm, and so in this respect was Rank with the object-relations theory, the interpersonal and even intersubjective point of view. He did even change epistemology quite explicitly; it is no longer a positivistic search for facts, as Freud's with the Wolf Man, but, as in his trauma theory, the introduction of the interpersonal element (the adult is silent and leaves the child alone with his problems, etc.). In this respect, Ferenczi was perhaps more an innovator—in other words, a heretic—than he himself would admit (a "secret rebel", as Clara Thompson [1944] called him), for reasons of loyalty and perhaps also through his incapacity for more venturesome self-assertion (except perhaps in his *Clinical Diary*—at least in the last year of his life). He worried too much about Freud's love. . . .

There were also differences regarding *therapeutic expectations*. Freud reproached Ferenczi even after his death (in the obituary) with having wanted to reach impossible aims, and Ferenczi reproached Freud in his *Diary* with talking down to his patients and treating them as "riffraff". "This was the point at which I would go no further with him" (Ferenczi, 1985 [1932], p. 249).

As in historical writing in general, it depends from what point of view we *question* the past. For anyone who today has his work model in *transference/countertransference*, in the here and now (like most analysts of today), Ferenczi is in fact a pioneer. The danger of this view is that Ferenczi is then seen as a solitary hero, without observing the historical context. On the other hand, for those who use Freud's one-person-psychology/metapsychology (1910–14) as a guide, Ferenczi might appear a heretic or dissident.

The concept of "dissidence", like many other concepts in the human sciences, is after all an *interpersonal* or interactive concept and depends not only on the subject's behaviour, but also on the screen of the observer's interpretation.

The differences with Adler and Jung became "deviant movements" because they had founded schools; Rank did not do so until much later, after his break with Freud, and Ferenczi did not do it at all.

The question of dissidence naturally brings up the question of *orthodoxy*, and we may wonder how far an orthodoxy existed at all. Freud himself worked every few years on new theoretical developments; and when he tries to define psychoanalysis he brings out only a few criteria (and somewhat differently at different points—

see "Psychoanalysis" and "Libido Theory", Freud, 1923a, p. 247, and F/Grod, 5.6.1917). If we limit orthodoxy to a few of these points, then orthodoxy has certainly *existed*, in the sense of "hypotheses of work", but if we look at Ferenczi's work, he also shared these hypotheses. Whether he was a dissident depends clearly on what is regarded or classified as orthodoxy, and if we look ourselves for that in Freud, we become embarrassed. (Today we must also note that as far as the question of orthodoxy is concerned, the situation is worse than in Freud's time: there are more local orthodoxies, a different one in every town, a Kleinian Latin-American orthodoxy, a Kleinian London orthodoxy, various Parisian orthodoxies, etc.). Aren't these orthodoxies organized around reigning cultural ideologies or around charismatic personalities?

We must also take into account that Freudianism was historically yet another of the "isms" that dominated the intellectual scene at the end of the nineteenth century, and one of those that were born in Vienna—Zionism and Austromarxism (both born in the Berggasse as well)—and others, such as Dadaism in Zürich, and so on. Most of them contain utopian promises of happiness, and thus features that simulate religions.

Freud looked for his disciples, not among his peer group but among those a few decades younger, some of whom had newly emigrated to Vienna—young intellectuals, to some extent uprooted, who saw the conquest of the *psyche* as the last step in the progress of enlightenment. Copernicus, Darwin, and Freud, as the latter has presented it (Freud, 1917a), spoke on these humiliations of human pride. The twentieth century was marked in individual matters by Freudianism, and in matters social by Marxism and Zionism. Dissidence would, accordingly, be everything that puts at risk the common aims of these movements—for Freud, the unconscious, the sexual, the infantile, and transference. At the beginning, the differences seem to have been partly masked; a century had to pass before the President of the IPA, Robert Wallerstein, could announce that we are in the midst of a *de facto* pluralism, "a pluralism of theoretical perspectives" (Wallerstein, 1988, p. 5).

CHAPTER NINE

Freud and Ferenczi:
a difficult friendship
or a tragic love affair?

Was the relationship between Freud and Ferenczi just simple friendship, with all the difficulties that may emerge in any human relationship, however amicable—or was it a love affair, with deeper-going expectations and passions, along with the inevitable deceptions that are part and parcel of those tragic longings and misunderstandings?

> On a saucer a cut-off—somewhat small and frail but firmly erect—male member is brought in, next to it some kinds of objects (eating utensils?). My younger brother has just cut off his penis in order to perform coitus (!). I think something like: that is not necessary. . . . (Fer/F, 20.12.1912)

This dream fragment is in a letter to Freud by Ferenczi—who has obstinately set his mind on making Freud analyse him. Incidentally, in a postscript to this letter he writes: "Today (on December 27) I feel significantly better. Hard to say whether my awareness of an improvement in my physical condition or this analysis was of more use" (Fer/F, 20.12.1912). He even makes a drawing so that Freud might understand him better. If one considers this an initial—or initiatory?—dream, one could speak of an *offer* in view of the wished-for analysis. So, from the beginning, there is an ambiguous friendship—a friendship in which one spends one's holidays together, but also a relationship between colleagues in which one discusses scientific topics and there is an analysis, with its display of multiple and inextricable transferences and countertransferences that can neither be resolved nor dissolved.

First episode:
a difficult friendship?

But let us go back to the beginning. As for the holidays, there are limitations right from the start: "It is understood at the outset that you will not disturb me in my work and that I won't have to take any precautions against you, but I can only look forward to discussing various things with you and not completely dispensing with meaningful association" (F/Fer, 10.05.1908).

Ferenczi's expectations regarding Freud are immense, and he develops a grandiose vision of how a small circle around Freud could collaborate on an "ideal level" (Ferenczi, 1911 [1910], p. 304), where "the father enjoyed no dogmatic authority, but only that to which he was entitled by reason of his abilities and labour" (p. 302)—a high ideal, indeed, particularly in the era of Franz Joseph and of Queen Victoria, and simultaneously a clear demand for the kind of relationship he wants.

As for Freud, he knows already on the occasion of their first holiday, as he writes to Jung, that his "travelling companion is a dear fellow, but dreamy in a disturbing kind of way, and his attitude towards me is infantile. . . . He has been too passive and receptive, letting everything be done for him like a woman, and I really haven't got enough homosexuality in me to accept him as one. These trips arouse a great longing for a real woman" (F/J, 24.9.1910). Ferenczi is submissive: "I am sorry that you had in me a travel companion who is still so much in need of education" (Fer/F, 28.9.1910). "[I]t was so terribly inconsiderate of me to want to spoil your vacation time by allowing myself to be educated by you" (Fer/F, 3.10.1910). This is a deep-rooted and far-reaching feeling: Ferenczi is even prepared for the possibility that Freud might reject him, prepared for a "situation in which, with respect to the disappointment that I caused you, you would no longer find it worthwhile to be interested in me" (Fer/F, 3.10.1910).

Ferenczi wants to be able to appear completely naked before the other. "My dream in which I saw you standing naked before me (naturally without feeling the slightest conscious—indeed, also in the dream still unconscious—sexual arousal) was the transparent symbolization of 1) the *ucs.* homosexual tendency and 2) the longing for absolute mutual openness" (Fer/F, 3.10.1910). "Just as in my relationship with Frau G. I strive for *absolute* mutual openness, in the same manner—and with even more justification—I believed that this, apparently cruel but in the end only useful, clear-as-day openness, which conceals nothing, could be possible in the relations between two ψα-minded people" (Fer/F, 3.10.1910). Narcissism mounts after the "withdrawal" of the homosexual libido, exactly as Freud describes it in this very correspondence, in alluding to Fliess and the Schreber case: "A piece of homosexual investment has been withdrawn and utilized for the enlargement of my own ego. I have succeeded where the paranoiac fails" (F/Fer, 6.10.1910).

The way is prepared for Freud's slip, writing that "I am that 'superman' whom we have constructed", instead of what the context would have required: "I am also not that 'superman'" (F/Fer, 6.10.1910).

Ferenczi comes to see that "I have also rather ruthlessly brought to light the resistance against my own homosexual drive components (and the uncommon sexual overestimation of women which goes along with it)" (Fer/F, 3.30.1910).

Little surprise, then, that Freud came to see Ferenczi's attempts at rebellion as inevitable:

> The result was that in Palermo, where he wanted to do the famous work on paranoia (Schreber) in collaboration with me, right on the first evening of work, when he wanted to dictate something to me, I rose up in a sudden burst of rebellion and explained that it was not at all a collaboration if he simply dictated to me. "So that's the way you are?"—he said, aston-

ished. "You perhaps wanted to take the whole thing?" Having said that, he worked alone every evening from then on, and I was left standing—I was choked with Bitterness. (Fer/Grod, 25.12.1921)

Is it really coincidence that they are working precisely on the subject of Schreber (Freud 1911c) and on the hypothesis that "the exciting cause of the illness was the appearance in him of a feminine (that is, a passive homosexual) wishful fantasy, which took as its object the figure of his doctor" (p. 47)?

This is the beginning of Ferenczi's search for a completely open and transparent relationship, of which he knows, however, "that the entire (unconsciously strengthened) homosexual drive component is behind it" (Fer/F, 3.10.1910).

Freud, for his part, is also preoccupied by his *own* "homosexual" problem—that is, with "Fliess's case, with the overcoming of which you just saw me occupied" (F/Fer, 6.10.1910). "My dreams at the time were ... entirely concerned with the Fliess matter" (6.10.1910).

Ferenczi seems to woo for love: "To dispense completely with your justified distrust of people (even of friends—after the Fliess case) and give yourself over to someone, e.g., an enthusiastic, impertinent youngster" (Fer/F, 3.10.1910). The "youngster" requests the older man's love, "not [to be] ashamed in front of each other, keep nothing secret, tell each other the truth without risk of insult or in the certain hope that within the truth there can be no lasting insult" (Fer/F, 3.10.1910)—a wish, indeed, for fusion, for symbiosis.

Freud often takes his distance, as on the occasion of Ferenczi's self-analytic letter, running over several pages, and containing the dream quoted above, to which he does not react. Often he writes: "Of course, I knew ... most of what you are writing about" (F/Fer, 6.10.1910). Did he really know nearly everything? Or rather: "I also haven't overcome the countertransference" (6.10.1910)? And this because of love: "I couldn't do it, just as I can't do it with my three sons because I like them" (6.10.1910). Thus, Ferenczi is adopted, he has become "the son" (neither a brother, nor an equal).

Second episode:
a difficult pair of analyst and analysand?

But Ferenczi is not (only) the "son", later he also becomes the *analysand*, and one cannot analyse, according to Freud, if one has not "overcome" the countertransference. The analyst has to "recognize this counter-transference in himself and overcome it" (1910c, pp. 144–145). Ferenczi insists: "I do not want to give up hope that you will let a part of your withdrawn homosexual libido be refloated and bring more sympathy to bear toward 'my ideal of honesty'" (Fer/F, 12.10.1910). He reasons:

> So how could I warm up to the fact that you extend your—in part, justified—distrust to the entire male sex! There is certainly much that is infantile in my yearning for honesty—but it certainly also has a healthy core.—Not everything that is infantile should be abhorred; for example, the child's urge for truth, which is only dammed up by false educational influences. [He adds a reference to Freud's own writings] (See Freud, 1910c; see also Freud's views on the enlightenment of children—etc.). (Fer/F, 12.10.1910)

Freud answers: "So, you are still asserting your point of view, and, I concede, ardently and with good arguments. But there is nothing obligatory [*Verbindliches*] in that" (F/Fer, 17.10.1910).

There is another side to Freud's attitude, as revealed in his confession: "I . . . am very much inclined toward plagiarism" (F/Fer, 8.2.1910). Ferenczi, in childlike enthusiasm, is in turn "pleased about your 'plagiarism' [*freue mich über Ihr 'Plagiat'*]" (Fer/F, 8.2.1910). Phantasizing about an exchange without limits. . . .

Ferenczi does not miss the clue—perhaps he wants to imitate the Master: "Jung is right when he urges me to gather young men around me whom I can teach and perhaps also love somewhat" (Fer/F, 5.4.1910). An advice to Freud?

All of this leads to a transition in the relationship, to an analysis with Freud, an analysis that even begins before it really starts. "I am sending you herewith a brief analysis of a dream for the *Zeitschrift*. I don't need to tell you beforehand that it comes from my self-analysis. . . . You will also recognize yourself in it—in the person of the doctor who doesn't want to analyze me" (Fer/F,

8.9.1914). After the first *tranche* of analysis: "I spent the . . . day . . . with self-analysis in writing. It went smoothly; I imagined I was talking to you" (Fer/F, 27.10.1914). In 1911, Freud publishes his work on Schreber's paranoia, and Ferenczi his own "On the Part Played by Homosexuality in the Pathogenesis of Paranoia".

There follows the episode with Elma, analysand of Ferenczi's, daughter of his mistress Gizella. Freud finally decides (!) against Elma, the young woman who could have given children to Ferenczi and, surprisingly, puts pressure on Ferenczi that he should choose Gizella, not Elma. Could this have something to do with jealousy? However this may be, for a long time Ferenczi will suffer from this conflict and its aftermath, complaining about depression and hypochondria, in spite of two more *tranches* of analysis in 1916 and in spite of the continuing idealization of Freud, as revealed, for example, in his repeated comparison of Freud with Goethe: "[I] found a correspondence, up to the smallest details, between Goethe's and your way of thinking and working, interests, worldview, type of disposition, so that I often wanted to cry out loud and call your name" (Fer/F, 4.4.1915). Ferenczi insists on this comparison even when Freud protests (F/Fer, 8.4.1915)—protests, however, that do not last long. Ferenczi writes: "Of all great men he is, incidentally, the only one who, I assume, would also not have been closed to ψα insights" (Fer/F, 4.4.1915). Freud echoes this in nearly the same terms: "I think that Goethe would not have rejected psycho-analysis in an unfriendly spirit. . . . He himself approached it at a number of points, recognized much through his own insight that we have since been able to confirm" (Freud, 1930a, p. 208). Ferenczi continues to insist on idealizing his analyst, making his point even clearer when speaking of "the benevolent and yet strict treatment of young initiates" (Fer/F, 21.4.1915) of Goethe and Freud. To put an end to this exchange of views on Goethe—and obviously also on himself—Freud declares: "On the whole, greatness doesn't weigh heavily upon me" (F/Fer, 23.4.1915).

This iridescence—or "mirror transference", as Kohut would later call it—has thus come to the fore, and the ties that have allowed the two writers to work on the subject of homosexuality have been reinforced by the idealizing narcissistic component— just as theory has it. This solution, however, cannot be a permanent one, not without the reappearance of melancholia, of depressive anxiety, and of hypochondriac traits that the ideal homosexual relationship was able to hide for some time. In order to find his place in this relationship, Ferenczi often has recourse to complaints, although there are some exceptions, for instance: "The hypochondriacal–melancholic ill humor has made room for a certain jollity" (Fer/F, 25.1.1922). The joys and sorrows of love?

Their rapprochement is of importance and becomes, according to Freud's later statement, "an intimate community of life, feeling, and interest" (F/Fer, 11.1.1933). It is touching to read Ferenczi's confession: "Earlier I was happy about an idea mostly as a favor to you" (Fer/F, 15.5.1922).

All of this, however, is not always easy. Ferenczi actually wants to be (symbiotically) on and in Freud's mind, even when Freud rejoins: "Now, as regards your effort to remain in harmony with me throughout, I value it highly as an expression of your friendship, but I find the goal neither necessary nor easily attainable" (F/Fer, 4.2.1924). He encourages Ferenczi: "I had hoped you would outgrow that childish role and take your place beside me as an associate and a peer. You have not . . ." (F/Fer, 2.10.1910). When Ferenczi, however, follows his own paths, Freud becomes more and more dissatisfied and suspects the end of the friendship or even treason—while at the same time pretending the opposite: "It does seem out of the question to me that either you or Rank, in your independent excursions, would ever abandon the ground of analysis" (F/Fer, 4.2.1924).

But the person of Ferenczi's analyst changes—or, better, doubles. After Freud, it is Groddeck. Precisely when Ferenczi enters into a therapeutic relationship with Groddeck, a kind of mutual analysis, Freud declares (moved, perhaps, by jealousy) that Groddeck's writings are "very German and bad" (F/Fer, 30.3.1922).

Third episode:
a difficult love affair?

In this quasi-ideal relationship between Freud and Ferenczi, more and more clouds appear on the horizon, however. The links between Ferenczi and Otto Rank and their joint book on *The Development of Psychoanalysis* [*Entwicklungsziele der Psychoanalyse*], as well as Rank's book of the same year (1924), *The Trauma of Birth*, place Freud in a difficult emotional and political situation. Karl Abraham and the Berliners, then also Ernest Jones, increasingly take a position of trenchant criticism, finally leading to the rupture with Rank. A genuine process of divorce ensues, with its to and fro, with its sulky withdrawals and its sentimental reconciliations, with its threats of rebellion and its repentant submissions, alternatingly following each other. In the end, this leads to the separation from a dear collaborator, a personal secretary, the editor of all the German-speaking psychoanalytic journals and head of the psychoanalytic publishing house, a man for whose studies at the university Freud had paid, a real son for some time—who, moreover, turns away like a prodigal son. . . . The image evoked in *Totem and Taboo* (1912/13) of the rebellion of the brother horde seems to come true once again in the immediate surroundings of Freud. He who looked for the links between homosexuality and paranoia will be faced with a paranoid atmosphere, seemingly related to questions of doctrine. Is this so because there are fundamental mechanisms at work that he had so brilliantly discovered and that inexorably operate in small groups, or is it, rather, that such images, fraught with meaning, work as "self-fulfilling prophecies"?

But Freud and Ferenczi have not yet reached that stage. There comes, first, Ferenczi's trip to America (1926/27) and Freud's confession that he needs Ferenczi and wants him to be near him and by his side—a trauma of separation. When Rank leaves Vienna, Freud writes melancholically: "Yes, Rank is gone from Vienna. . . . The main thing . . . is that he has now carried out in a so to speak sober, cold way what he originally wanted to achieve . . .: loosing himself from me and from all of us" (F/Fer, 23.4.1926). Does he fear the same from Ferenczi's departure?

Probably to furnish himself with an explanation, this is also when Freud forms the idea that Rank is ill, that Rank has a "neurosis, which has become manifest" (F/Fer, 4.9.1924). Later, Freud's disciples will understand, and Ferenczi, too, will be considered ill. If someone is not in accordance with Freud's insight in this elitist group, the Secret Committee, he is declared to have neurotic resistances and is therefore ill. At the same time, this serves the purpose of fighting against those who put forward different ideas—because the ideas of a sick person cannot be of full value.

Let us note the fact that the frequency of letters in the third volume of the Freud/Ferenczi correspondence is much less than in the two preceding ones. Whereas during the 14 years comprised in the third volume they exchanged some 413 letters, in the six years of 1908 to 1914 alone they had written 526.

When Ferenczi plans to write on thought transference, linked to the problem of countertransference, Freud answers: "I advise you against it. Don't do it. . . . With it you would throw a bomb into the psychoanalytic edifice, which will certainly not fail to explode" (F/Fer, 20.3.1925).

Here we witness one of those small cuts that will eventually dig an ever deeper ditch between the technical and theoretical views of Freud and Ferenczi (note how carefully Freud weighs his words: "You are distancing yourself from me more and more. I say . . . not: alienating" (F/Fer, 18.9.1931). Ferenczi's technical experiments, his active therapy and method of relaxation, his interest in traumatism, his intensification of the cure, as in the case of R.N., the rediscovery of the role played by the trauma, with accompanying mechanisms such as disavowal, splitting, identification with the aggressor, and particularly the decisive role of countertransference—all of these lead to a theoretical model that would become that of object relations and intersubjectivity.

Freud does not follow Ferenczi. Needless to say, some elements of this development are linked to Ferenczi's analytic experience with Freud. When he speaks of "the restrained coolness" (Ferenczi, 1933 [294], p. 159) of the analyst, does he not also speak of his own feelings towards Freud the analyst? Again, when he says that the analysand has "an ardent desire to get rid of this oppressive love" (p. 164), does he not also speak of his desire to get rid of Freud's love? To be sure, this rings a bell in Freud: "I don't any longer believe that you will rectify yourself. . . . For three years you have been systematically turning away from me, probably developed a personal hostility" (F/Fer, 2.10.1932). In the end, according to Freud, this is nobody's fault, and certainly not his own: "Some psychological misfortune or other has brought it about in you" (F/Fer, 11.1.1933). Is the analyst Freud giving up analytic understanding?

But there does remain some of the love. One of Ferenczi's last letters (29.03.1933) shows him concerned that Freud should take himself to a place of security from the mounting national-socialism (". . . I advise you to take advantage of what time remains, since the situation is not imminently threatening, to leave for a more stable country, England, for example. Take some patients with you and your daughter Anna"—Fer/F, 29.3.1933)—which, incidentally, also shows that he had a sound judgement of the political situation and that he was not crazy at all, as Jones alleges. Freud's answer: It is more important to me for you to regain your health ("The difference between us . . . can wait . . ., it is more important to me that you should recover your health"—F/Fer, 2.4.1933). As for Ferenczi, he comes back to the love he had felt for Freud, not without bitter self-criticism, considering that he had "arrived at 'obsequiousness' (Liebesdienerei)" towards the strong man Freud was in his eyes. He realized that his enthusiasm had already diminished by the time when he went to America. Now he reaches the conclusion—"the last disappointment"—that Freud "does not love anyone, only himself and his work" (Ferenczi, 1985 [1932], p. 160; for the semantic field of this word: "*Liebesdienerin*" = lady of the night, prostitute; "*Liebesdienst*" = labour or service of love = sexual favour).

The history of this development has been written by Judith Dupont in her introduction to the third volume of the *Freud/ Ferenczi Correspondence*; Ernst Falzeder also deals with this topic. So, instead of entering into the details of these theoretical and technical problems, let me just state that, when Ferenczi takes off for America for ten months, from September 1926 to the spring of 1927, the rupture in their relationship deepens. Freud tolerates the geographical separation poorly. He has to cope with this separation just shortly after he had theoretically played down the fundamental importance of this factor in his controversy with Rank—only to rehabilitate it immediately afterwards in the guise of "separation anxiety" (in the appendix of *Inhibitions, Symptoms and Anxiety*, published in the same year, 1926). Freud expresses great reservations regarding Ferenczi's travel plans to America: "I can only hope that this journey will not signify the disappointment that some predict" (F/Fer, 6.6.1926). Ferenczi considers it to "be a time of weaning for me and for my wife" (Fer/F, 30.5.1926), and he reminds Freud of the possibility that after America he might move from Budapest to Vienna. "Time of weaning"—does this only reflect Ferenczi's conscious thoughts, or is it also a "weaning" from Europe and from Freud, in search of greater freedom? However consciously a text is written, the unconscious is always its co-author. . . . There will certainly be moments of rapprochement—for example, when Ferenczi offers to analyse Freud, stricken by cancer: "Many thanks for your touching suggestion" (F/Fer, 27.2.1926). Ferenczi understands only too well the reason for this refusal: "I find it actually tragic that you, who endowed the world with psychoanalysis, find it so difficult to be—indeed, are not at all—in a position to entrust yourself to anyone" (Fer/F, 26.2.1926). This tallies with his later, somewhat pathetic question: "My . . . hope extends to the point where an also analytically free talking things out can be possible, even between old friends. . . . Do you consider such mutual openness impossible?" (Fer/F, 14.2.1930).

Ferenczi says goodbye to Freud in the latter's retreat on the Semmering, where he recuperates, always ready to make the short train ride back to Vienna and his doctors. Jones remarks gloomily: "It was the last occasion on which Freud felt really happy in Ferenczi's company" (Jones, 1957, p. 126). In America, Ferenczi defends lay analysis: "In this question I identify (as Jones says) too much with you, Herr Professor" (Fer/F, 30.6.1927). He becomes melancholic himself and reminisces about their former journey together, in 1909, "the sunny days on board" (Fer/F, 27.9.1926). The two former friends and pupils of Freud who dwell in the United States—Rank in the Old School and Ferenczi in the New School for Social Research—will, incidentally, not meet.

Their exchange dwindles during the following years, just as the theory of homosexuality–paranoia predicts, which perhaps lets Freud relive his experience with Fliess. Ferenczi, for his part, becomes more and more aware of the paranoia that surrounds him. Already in 1910 he had recognized "the pathology of such associations" as the International Psychoanalytical Association, which he had helped to found, and he was "aware that in most political, social and scientific organizations childish megalomania, vanity, admiration of empty formalities, blind obedience, or personal egoism prevail instead of quiet, honest work in the general interest" (Ferenczi, 1911 [79], p. 302).

The tone of the correspondence worsens and sometimes becomes outright harsh. The infamous episode of the "kissing technique" (Ferenczi, 1985 [1932], p. 45) obviously does not help either (F/Fer, 13.12.1931; Fer/F, 27.12.1931). In his *Clinical Diary*, Ferenczi reveals that Clara Thompson boasted: "I can kiss Papa Ferenczi as often as I like", and that her statement was reported to Freud (Ferenczi 1985 [1932], p. 45). In his own words, Ferenczi treats "this distasteful incident" with "total indifference". Only later does he become aware of the transferential implications of his patient's behaviour. "As a child, her father . . . had indulged in extensive sexual play with her . . . and she sought revenge by 'denouncing him'" (pp. 46–47).

More and more, however, Ferenczi is on his guard and takes an independent stance. He tells Freud that he is dissatisfied with him—for instance: "I am pleased to hear that you find my new views 'very ingenious'; I would have been much more pleased if you had declared them to be correct, probable, or even only plausible" (Fer/F, 21.9.1930).

When Freud declares that he is "fed up" (F/Fer, 11.1.1930) with psychoanalysis as a therapy as well as with patients in general (to whom he refers as "riff-raff"; cf. Ferenczi, 1985 [1932], 12.6.1932), does that also mean the end of the love he has for his friends, and for psychoanalysis?

In fact, loving relationships with men come to an end. The Secret Committee breaks apart, and women take its place: Anna Freud, Minna Bernays, Lou Andreas-Salomé, Marie Bonaparte, Dorothy Tiffany-Burlingham, Ruth Mack-Brunswick (to whom Freud also entrusts the famous Wolf Man after the latter's analysis with him).

Ferenczi continues on his way in his experiences with difficult patients. He actually becomes a haven for lost causes. He no longer wants to do administrative work and to hold positions of power, such as the presidency of the IPA—and this despite the great pressure put on him by Freud himself, who even speaks of the "struggle of men" into which Ferenczi *should* enter instead of staying on "the island of dreams", playing with his "fantasy-children" (F/Fer, undated, #1216). Such work is no longer of interest to Ferenczi, and it would probably also demand too much loyalty—beyond the limits of his evolution towards more freedom.

Parting

Is there an echo in Freud's mind of what he had written about transference love (Freud 1915a, p. 157) when he states that for the doctor the phenomenon signifies a useful warning against any tendency to developing a countertransference? Freud also requires that the physician must recognize that the patient's falling in love is induced by the analytic situation. The analytic technique, according to Freud, demands that the physician should deny the patient, craving love, the satisfaction he or she demands. In his view, ethical as well as technical reasons prevent the doctor from giving the patient this love. But was Freud's and Ferenczi's relationship really an analytic one? Was it not mixed up with other factors? And was this mixing-up perhaps the source of suffering in which both were involved and by which they were bound?

Is this the story of the woes of an undissolved transference—indeed, transference love? It might, rather, be a question of definition whether we can talk of mere friendship?

The psychoanalytic community has poorly tolerated looking its own history in the face. Instead, it has preferred, in utmost loyalty and in a soothing need for exaggerated idealization, to deprive itself of the contributions of original thinkers—among them Sándor Ferenczi. What he had written was, in fact, not written at all—he never existed, for instance, for the APA-linked North-American institutes! Therefore one had to rediscover the importance of traumatism (for instance, via Masud Khan), rediscover interaction and intersubjectivity in the work of Klein, Winnicott, Sullivan, and various schools around the world, rediscover splitting and borderline structures in Kernberg's theory, and rediscover that "something more than interpretation" goes with interpretation, as Daniel Stern put it recently (in Williams, 1999, p. 197). This loss should be sufficient reason to have a fresh, close look at what really happened in our history. *Drôle d'histoire*—a funny history—a history to meditate on. . . .

* * *

Is this the end of a long scientific collaboration, of an intense friendship at the limit of passion, and also the end of an analytic relationship that Ferenczi would, without doubt, have wanted to be different from what it became? We have reasons to suppose that this is not the real end: Freud seems to have been obliged to let pass a time of mourning, from 1933 to the end of 1937. Then, in 1937, three times the name of, and the topics raised by, Ferenczi and the theme of trauma come up again in "Analysis Terminable and Interminable" (1937c). As if Freud had been rethinking Ferenczi's ideas, in 1938, in the *Outline of Psychoanalysis* (1940a [1938]—published only posthumously), Freud states that the effect of the castration threat is the greatest *trauma*. Here he evidently combines his theory—to which he is very much attached—of the Oedipus complex and the castration threat with the theory of trauma which, he feared, in the context of the discussion of Rank's theory of birth trauma, could endanger the central position of the castration threat. Now Freud proposes a kind of synthesis. In 1939, he takes the whole question up again in *Moses and Monotheism* (1939a) and develops for the first time the concept of trauma in relation to narcissism and the early injuries of the ego (*narcissistic modification*, p. 74). The early traumatic injuries are seen as narcissistic wounds that leave the ego "too fragile". Remembering that Ferenczi was in fact the first to put forward the concept of the impact of early trauma with ensuing splits and concomitant disturbances of narcissism, we can see Freud taking up Ferenczi's ideas in *Moses and Monotheism* (1939a). The establishment of an enclave in the psyche ("a State within the State", p. 76) shows how the trauma completes its work of destruction. He is opening in the wake of Ferenczi the problems of early narcissistic injuries, of splitting, of deficiencies in symbolizing as the later evolution of psychoanalytic theory has it in the 1940s and 1950s and 1960s, under the headlines "early disturbances", so-called "borderline states", and "heavily traumatized patients' pathology". . . .

Ferenczi was at the beginning of a still endless evolution.

CHAPTER TEN

Ferenczi's legacy

Having reviewed the history of Ferenczi's ideas and personality with reference to the *nodal points* of his thought and to his principal *relationships*—specifically, that with Sigmund Freud—we ought now to be in a position to bring our account to a close. However, it soon becomes evident that a clearcut, definitive conclusion with fixed boundaries is not possible. This man was made to stimulate us. The idea of founding a school and encouraging people to act in the way that he, Ferenczi, thought correct was abhorrent to him. He wanted to influence others to live their private and professional lives *in their own way*. In his wake there was to be no school or institution, but instead an incitement to think, to feel, to have emotions, and to ask questions. His legacy is therefore found to have infiltrated the whole of psychoanalytic thought, impressing its stamp sometimes firmly—as with the British "Middle Group" of analysts or the American interpersonal school—and sometimes less so. There are also some surprising instances: for example, Jacques Lacan, who is certainly not known for his use of references, explicitly quotes him in his well-known pun on Ferenczi's name *"faire ainsi"* (these words, pronounced identically to "Ferenczi" in French, mean "to do it this way"); and Lacan—who seldom acknowledged any merit in other analysts unless they belonged to his own school—also respected Ferenczi's pupil Balint. Astonishing tributes flowed, too, from the pens of Anna Freud and others from whom one would not immediately have expected either sympathy or recognition. This, then, was the ultimate fate of his *œuvre*—to infiltrate the field of psychoanalysis in the absence of a school that specifically invoked his name (with a few exceptions). This was, indeed, an astounding psychoanalyst, in an environment where apprenticeship in a master–pupil relationship was the chief means of transmission. An analyst like him—an analyst unlike any other—is badly, sorely needed.

Ferenczi's ideas have played a major role in influencing our present psychoanalytic theory and practice. They have been brought to the United Kingdom mainly by Michael Balint, falling on fertile ground in the British "Middle Group". Balint was indebted to Ferenczi in numerous ways: his notion of the "basic fault", in particular, was a further development of Ferenczi's "confusion of tongues" (cf. Falzeder, 1986), his concept of the three phases of the trauma was a paraphrase of Ferenczi's ideas, and even his work with general practitioners had been anticipated by Ferenczi. Paula Heimann and Margaret Little took up Ferenczi's stress on countertransference. Melanie Klein's concepts of the depressive position and of reparation remind one of Ferenczi's seeing the traumatized child as the adult's "psychiatrist", and her very influential conception of projective identification (Klein, 1946a) has its roots in Ferenczi's work—certainly not in Abraham's—as do the works of Rosenfeld and Wilfred Bion (indeed, Bion initiated a contribution to the metapsychology of the analyst's thought processes as it was outlined by Ferenczi). Winnicott's term, the "transitional object", had been anticipated by Ferenczi (cf. Ferenczi, 1928 [281], p. 67), as had his accent on the importance of the caregiver's personality, his fight against dogmatism, his therapeutic use of "regression to dependency", his concepts of "impingement", of the impact of birth, and of the "true" and "false self". "Ferenczi's concept of 'primary object love'", comments Harry Guntrip, "prepared the way for the later work of Melanie Klein, Fairbairn, Balint, Winnicott, and all others who today recognize that object-relations start at the beginning in the infant's needs for the mother" (Fuller,

1985, p. 14). It is interesting, incidentally, that Ferenczi analysed leading figures of British psychoanalysis, such as Ernest Jones, Melanie Klein, Michael Balint, Barbara Lantos, David Eder, and John Rickman (also an analysand of Freud's, who would himself, in turn, become analyst to Enid Balint, Wilfred Bion, and Masud Khan).

It is well known that Anna Freud was critical of some directions taken by psychoanalysis in Ferenczi's footsteps. It is less well known, however, that she, nevertheless, highly valued not only Ferenczi the man, but also his controversial ideas and experiments. To her friend Eva Rosenfeld she wrote in 1931 that "any modification of strict analysis is something which surely requires a widely experienced analyst, thoroughly steeped in analysis (like Ferenczi, or Aichhorn, or possibly Simmel . . .)" [letter, summer 1931; in Heller, 1992, p. 160). Shortly afterwards, Anna Freud wrote to Lou Andreas-Salomé: "It is not troubling as long as this method is confined to Ferenczi, for he has the necessary restraint for it. But others should not do it" (29 November 1931; in Young-Bruehl, 1988, p. 194). But perhaps her most concise statement about Ferenczi is found in her letter to Michael Balint of 23.5.1935:

> Sometimes I feel that some [misunderstandings] arise from the idea we would not value Ferenczi as highly as you and your friends in Budapest do. I beg you not to believe this. If there is a person without whom psychoanalysis would be unthinkable, who, for me, is inseparably connected with psychoanalysis as such, it is Ferenczi. My esteem and admiration for his personality date back very far, to times when you cannot even have known him yet. [23.5.1935; unpublished; Balint Archives, Geneva; translated for this edition]

It is not surprising that a central term of Anna Freud's, "developmental lines", stems from Ferenczi (Ferenczi, 1911 [75], p. 139), as well as the idea of identification with the aggressor (Ferenczi, 1985 [1932] p. 190).

In North America, Ferenczi's contributions were haughtily ignored by the principal current, ego-psychology. This is not surprising, as Ferenczi warned of the dangers attendant upon an overly emphasized and unilateral ego-psychology: "The critical opinion, which has been forming in me during this period, is that psychoanalysis practices in far too unilateral a fashion . . . a psychology of the Ego" (Fer/F, 25.12.1929). The fact that Géza Roheim, in New York, had dedicated his monumental *Psychoanalysis and Anthropology* (Roheim, 1950) to the memory of Sándor Ferenczi may have contributed to the fact that until recently Roheim had remained virtually unknown in psychoanalytic circles in his country of adoption. Franz Alexander in Chicago and Sándor Rado in New York did return to some aspects of the Ferenczi heritage, notably through their interest in technique and their taste for innovation. Franz Alexander himself wrote that Ferenczi's and Rank's ideas in their joint book (1924) had led him to try out fewer analytic sessions and see the value of emotional reliving in transference (Alexander & Selesnick, 1966, p. 249). John N. Rosen has taken up Ferenczi's technique of the "dramatic dialogue" in therapy (Rosen, 1946, 1947).

It is Clara Thompson—Ferenczi's (and Erich Fromm's) analysand and herself the analyst of Harry Stack Sullivan—who can be considered his main direct successor on the North American continent, through her general orientation and, more specifically, through her articles on countertransference and the role of the analyst's personality (Thompson, 1956). Thompson had personal analysis with Ferenczi in Budapest during the summers of 1928 and 1929, and for two years continuously from 1931 until Ferenczi's death in 1933. In an unpublished paper, Thompson (1955) attributed to Sullivan her decision to seek analysis from Ferenczi: ". . . I would not have gone to Ferenczi, because who would have the nerve to go to Budapest all alone, if Sullivan hadn't insisted that this was the only analyst in Europe he had any confidence in, and therefore, if I was going to Europe and get analyzed I had just better go there. So, I went." It would appear that Sullivan had been much impressed by Ferenczi's address on "Present-Day Problems in Psychoanalysis" before the American Psychoanalytic Association at its Christmas meeting in 1926. After this presentation, which emphasized the practical aspects of ego psychology, Sullivan, I. Coriat, and H. W. Frink had engaged in a lengthy discussion (Noble & Burnham, 1969, p. 30). In April 1927 Ferenczi presented his paper on "The Genital Theory" before the Washington Psychopathological Society. "It appears that Ferenczi spent considerable time in Washington that winter [1927], since, under the auspices of the Washington Psychoanalytic Association, he gave a series of seminars at the home of Philip Graven" (Noble & Burnham, 1969, p. 15). (In 1930, William Alanson White was president, Clara Thompson vice-president, and Ben Karpman secretary of the Washington Psychoanalytic Association; Harry Stack Sullivan was still vice-president of the American Psychoanalytic Association.)

In studying the vicissitudes of psychoanalytic ideas and theories, whether we know it or not, we return surprisingly often to Ferenczi. Further research might allow us to specify his impact more clearly, but already we can state without exaggeration that his legacy is with us, whether or not we are aware of it.

The book on psychoanalytic practice that Freud had intended to write, but which was never to see the light of day—*The Method of Psychoanalysis*—was in fact composed implicitly by Ferenczi during the course of his *œuvre*. Throughout his life and on the basis of his experiences, he wrote, corrected, and rewrote it. Present-day psychoanalytic technique, the importance assigned to the transference and the countertransference, the part played by the analyst, the role of the mother and of trauma: all this comes from Ferenczi—none of it is in Freud. The entire psychoanalytic community adheres to these notions, while acknowledging only a part of Ferenczi's legacy. The discovery of the other parts that still lie in the shadows is a task for the twenty-first century, the new century of psychoanalysis, which will, it is to be hoped, be the century of the *Clinical Diary* and the *Correspondence*. Freud (1933c) wrote that Ferenczi had made all psychoanalysts his pupils, and this may now come to pass.

REFERENCES AND BIBLIOGRAPHY

Aron, L., & Harris, A. (Eds.) (1993). *The Legacy of Sándor Ferenczi.* Hillsdale, NJ: Analytic Press.

Ackerknecht, E. H. (1957). Josef Breuer über seinen Anteil an der Psychoanalyse. *Gesnerus, 14:* 169–171.

Alexander, F. G., & Selesnick, S. T. (1966). *The History of Psychiatry.* New York: Harper & Row.

Andreas-Salomé, L. (1964 [1912–13]). *The Freud Journal of Lou Andreas-Salomé.* London: Hogarth Press.

Balint, M. (1933a). On transference of emotions. In: *Primary Love and Psychoanalytic Technique* (second, enlarged edition) (pp. 165–177). London: Tavistock.

Balint, M. (1933e). Character analysis and new beginning. In: *Primary Love and Psychoanalytic Technique* (second, enlarged edition) (pp. 151–164). London: Tavistock.

Balint, M. (1934b). Ferenczi Sándor mint orvos. *Gyógyászat, 74:* 312–315.

Balint, M. (1949a). Dr Sándor Ferenczi, obiit 1933. *International Journal of Psycho-Analysis, 30* (4), 215–219. Reprinted in: *Problems of Human*

Pleasure and Behaviour. Classic Essays in Humanistic Psychiatry (pp. 243–250). New York: Liveright, 1956.

Balint, M. (1956a). *Problems of Human Pleasure and Behaviour. Classic Essays in Humanistic Psychiatry*. New York: Liveright.

Balint, M. (1964g). Preface to: Ferenczi, S. *Psychanalyse, Vol. 1* (pp. 7–11). Paris: Payot, 1968; rev. ed. 1982.

Balint, M. (1965a). *Primary Love and Psychoanalytic Technique* (second, enlarged edition). London: Tavistock.

Balint, M. (1968a). *The Basic Fault. Therapeutic Aspects of Regression.* London: Tavistock.

Balint, M. (1969a). Trauma and object relationship. *International Journal of Psycho-Analysis, 50* (4): 429–435.

Balint, M. (1969i). Introduction to: S. Ferenczi, *Journal clinique (January–October 1932)* (pp. 13–15). Paris: Payot, 1985.

Balint, M., & Balint, A. (1939a). On transference and countertransference. *International Journal of Psycho-Analysis, 20* (3–4): 223–230; reprinted in: M. Balint, *Primary Love and Psychoanalytic Technique* (second, enlarged edition) (pp. 201–208). London: Tavistock.

Barande, I. (1972). *Sándor Ferenczi*. Paris: Payot.

Bertrand, M., Bokanowski, T., et al. (1994): *Ferenczi, patient et psychanalyste.* Paris: L'Harmattan.

Binswanger, L. (1956). *Erinnerungen an Sigmund Freud*. Bern: Francke.

Blanton, S. (1971). *Diary of my Analysis with Sigmund Freud*. New York: Hawthorn Books.

Bokanowski, T. (1997). *Sándor Ferenczi*. Paris: Presses Universitaires de France.

Bokanowski, T. et al. (Eds.) (1995). *Sándor Ferenczi*. Monographies de la Revue Française de Psychanalyse, Paris: Presses Universitaires de France.

Brome, V. (1982). *Ernest Jones, Freud's Alter Ego*. London: Caliban Books.

Carotenuto, A. (Ed.) (1981). *A Secret Symmetry. Sabina Spielrein Between Freud and Jung*. London: Routledge & Kegan Paul, 1984.

Chertok, L. (1983). Psychotherapie und Sexualität. *Psychoanalyse, 4* (1): 2–20.

Cremerius, J. (1983). "Die Sprache der Zärtlichkeit und der Leidenschaft": Reflexionen zu Sándor Ferenczis Wiesbadener Vortrag von 1932. *Psyche, 37* (11): 988–1015.

Decker, H. (1991). *Freud, Dora, and Vienna 1900*. New York: The Free Press.

Deutsch, H. (1926). Occult processes occurring during psychoanalysis. In: G. Devereux (Ed.), *Psychoanalysis and the Occult*. New York: International Universities Press, 1953.

Dupont, J. (1985). Introduction. In: S. Ferenczi: *The Clinical Diary* (pp. xi–xvii). Cambridge, MA: Harvard University Press, 1988.

Erös, F., & Giampieri, P. (1987). The beginnings of the reception of psychoanalysis in Hungary: 1900–1920. *Sigmund Freud House Bulletin, 11* (2): 13–27.

Études Freudiennes (1993). *Freud–Ferenczi. Chronique d'une correspondance, 34* (September).

Falzeder, E. (1986). *Die "Sprachverwirrung" und die "Grundstörung". Die Untersuchungen S. Ferenczis und M. Balints über Entstehung und Auswirkungen früher Objektbeziehungen*. Salzburg, Austria: Salzburger Sozialisationsstudien, No. 10.

Ferenczi, S. (1899). Spiritizmus. *Gyógyászat, 39* (23 July), 30: 477–479.

Ferenczi, S. (1901). A szerelem a tudományban. *Gyógyászat, 41* (24 March), 12: 190–192.

Ferenczi, S. (1902). Homosexualitas feminina. *Gyógyászat, 42* (16 March), 11: 167–168.

Ferenczi, S. (1904a). A villamosság mint gyógyszer. *Gyógyászat, 44* (10 January), 2: 20–21.

Ferenczi, S. (1904b). A hypnosis gyógyító értékéröl. *Gyógyászat, 44* (25 December), 52: 820–822.

Ferenczi, S. (1908 [60]). Actual- and psychoneuroses in the light of Freud's investigations and psycho-analysis. In: *Further Contributions to the Theory and Technique of Psycho-Analysis* (pp. 30–55). London: Hogarth Press, 1959 (reprinted London: Karnac Books, 1980).

Ferenczi, S. (1908 [63]). Psychoanalysis and education. In: *Final Contributions to the Problems and Methods of Psycho-Analysis* (pp. 299–307). London: Hogarth Press, 1955 (reprinted London: Karnac Books, 1980).

Ferenczi, S.: (1909 [67]). Introjection and transference. In: *First Contributions to Psycho-Analysis* (pp. 35–93). London: Hogarth Press, 1955 (reprinted London: Karnac Books, 1980).

Ferenczi S. (1911 [75]). On obscene words. Contribution to the psychology of the latent period. In: *First Contributions to Psycho-Analysis* (pp. 132–153). London: Hogarth Press, 1955 (reprinted London: Karnac Books, 1980).

Ferenczi, S. (1911 [1910] [79]). On the organisation of the psycho-analytic movement. In: *Final Contributions to the Problems and Methods of Psycho-Analysis* (pp. 299–307). London: Hogarth Press, 1955 (reprinted London: Karnac Books, 1980).

Ferenczi, S. (1911 [80]). On the part played by homosexuality in the pathogenesis of paranoia. In: *First Contributions to Psycho-Analysis* (pp. 154–184). London: Hogarth Press, 1955 (reprinted London: Karnac Books, 1980).

Ferenczi, S. (1912 [85]). Transitory symptom-constructions during the analysis. In: *First Contributions to Psycho-Analysis* (pp. 193–212). London: Hogarth Press, 1955 (reprinted London: Karnac Books, 1980).

Ferenczi, S. (1913 [105]). To whom does one relate one's dreams? In: *Further Contributions to the Theory and Technique of Psycho-Analysis* (p. 349). London: Hogarth Press, 1955 (reprinted London: Karnac Books, 1980).

Ferenczi, S. (1913 [114]. A little Chanticleer. In: *First Contributions to Psycho-Analysis* (pp. 240–252). London: Hogarth Press, 1955 (reprinted London: Karnac Books, 1980).

Ferenczi, S. (1914 [139]). Falling asleep during the analysis. In: *Further Contributions to the Theory and Technique of Psycho-Analysis* (pp. 249–250). London: Hogarth Press, 1955 (reprinted London: Karnac Books, 1980).

Ferenczi, S. (1914 [145]). The "forgetting" of a symptom and its explanation in a dream. In: *Further Contributions to the Theory and Technique of Psycho-Analysis* (pp. 412–413). London: Hogarth Press, 1955 (reprinted London: Karnac Books, 1980).

Ferenczi, S. (1914 [147]). Discontinuous analysis. In: *Further Contributions to the Theory and Technique of Psycho-Analysis* (pp. 233–235). London: Hogarth Press, 1955 (reprinted London: Karnac Books, 1980).

Ferenczi, S. (1915 [159]). Psychogenic anomalies of voice production. In: *Further Contributions to the Theory and Technique of Psycho-Analysis* (pp. 233–235). London: Hogarth Press, 1955 (reprinted London: Karnac Books, 1980).

Ferenczi, S. (1915 [181]). Besprechung von: J. Kollarits. Contribution à l'étude des rêves. In: *Bausteine zur Psychoanalyse*, Vol. 4. Bern, Huber, 1964 (no English translation).

Ferenczi, S. (1917 [199]). Barátságom Schächter Miksával [My friendship with Miksa Schächter]. *Gyógyászat, 31.* [*La mia amicizia con Miksa Schächter. Scritti preanalitici 1899–1908.* ed. J. Mészaros & M. Casonato. Turin: Bollati Boringhieri, 1992] (no English translation).

Ferenczi, S. (1924 [268]). Thalassa: a theory of genitality. *Psychoanalytic Quarterly, 2* (1933): 361–403; *3* (1933): 1–29, 200–222.

Ferenczi, S. (1926 [271]). Contra-indications to the "active" psychoanalytical technique. In: *Further Contributions to the Theory and Technique of Psycho-Analysis* (pp. 217–230). London: Hogarth Press, 1955 (reprinted London: Karnac Books, 1980).

Ferenczi, S. (1928 [281]). The adaptation of the family to the child. In: *Final Contributions to the Problems and Methods of Psycho-Analysis* (pp. 61–76). London: Hogarth Press, 1955 (reprinted London: Karnac Books, 1980).

Ferenczi, S. (1928 [283]). The elasticity of psycho-analytical technique. In: *Final Contributions to the Problems and Methods of Psycho-Analysis* (pp. 87–101). London: Hogarth Press, 1955 (reprinted London: Karnac Books, 1980).

Ferenczi, S. (1928 [306]). Über der Lehrgang des Psychoanalytikers. In: *Bausteine zur Psychoanalyse, vol. 3: Arbeiten aus den Jahren 1908–1933.* Bern, Huber, 1964, pp. 422–431 (no English translation).

Ferenczi, S. (1930 [291]). The principle of relaxation and neocatharsis. In: *Final Contributions to the Problems and Methods of Psycho-Analysis* (pp. 108–125). London: Hogarth Press, 1955 (reprinted London: Karnac Books, 1980).

Ferenczi, S. (1931 [292]). Child analysis in the analysis of adults. In: *Final Contributions to the Problems and Methods of Psycho-Analysis* (pp. 126–142). London: Hogarth Press, 1955 (reprinted London: Karnac Books, 1980).

Ferenczi, S. (1933 [293]). Freud's influence on medicine. In: *Final Contributions to the Problems and Methods of Psycho-Analysis* (pp. 143–155). London: Hogarth Press, 1955 (reprinted London: Karnac Books, 1980).

Ferenczi, S. (1933 [294]). Confusion of tongues between adults and the child. In: *Final Contributions to the Problems and Methods of Psycho-*

Analysis (pp. 156–167). London: Hogarth Press, 1955 (reprinted London: Karnac Books, 1980).

Ferenczi, S. (1933 [308]). On the Revision of the Interpretation of Dreams. In: *Final Contributions to the Problems and Methods of Psycho-Analysis* (pp. 238–242). London: Hogarth Press, 1955 (reprinted London: Karnac Books, 1980).

Ferenczi, S. (1938 [1920–1932][308]). Notes and fragments. In: *Final Contributions to the Problems and Methods of Psycho-Analysis* (pp. 216–279). London: Hogarth Press, 1955 (reprinted London: Karnac Books).

Ferenczi, S. (1985 [1932]). *The Clinical Diary of Sándor Ferenczi*. Cambridge, MA: Harvard University Press.

Ferenczi, S., & Groddeck, G. (1982). *Briefwechsel 1921–1933*. Frankfurt/M.: Fischer, 1986.

Ferenczi, S., & Rank, O. (1924). *The Development of Psychoanalysis*. New York and Washington, DC, Nervous and Mental Disease Publishing Co., 1925. Reprinted Madison, CT: International Universities Press, 1986.

Fischer, D. (1977). *Les analysés parlent*. Paris: Stock.

Freud, S. (1893h), with J. Breuer. On the psychical mechanism of hysterical phenomena: A lecture. *Standard Edition*, 3: 25–39.

Freud, S. (1894a). The neuro-psychoses of defence. *S.E.*, 3: 41–61.

Freud, S. (1895d), with J. Breuer. *Studies on Hysteria*. *S.E.*, 2.

Freud, S. (1896b). Further remarks on the neuro-psychoses of defence. *S.E.*, 3: 157–185.

Freud, S. (1900a). *The Interpretation of Dreams*. *S.E.*, 4–5.

Freud, S. (1901b). *The Psychopathology of Everyday Life*. *S.E.*, 6.

Freud, S. (1905a). On psychotherapy. *S.E.*, 7: 255–268.

Freud, S. (1905c). *Jokes and Their Relation to the Unconscious*. *S.E.*, 7.

Freud, S. (1905e [1901]). Fragment of an analysis of a case of hysteria. *S.E.*, 7: 1–122.

Freud, S. (1907a [1906]). *Delusions and Dreams in Jensen's "Gradiva"*. *S.E.*, 9: 1–95.

Freud, S. (1909b). Analysis of a phobia in a five-year-old boy. *S.E.*, 10: 1–147.

Freud, S. (1909d). Notes upon a case of obsessional neurosis. *S.E.*, 10: 151–249.

Freud, S. (1910a [1909]). Five lectures on psycho-analysis. *S.E.*, 11: 1–55.

Freud, S. (1910c). *Leonardo da Vinci and a Memory of His Childhood. S.E.,* 11: 59.

Freud, S. (1910d). The future prospects of psycho-analytic therapy. *S.E., 11:* 139–151.

Freud, S. (1911c). Psycho-analytic notes on an autobiographical account of a case of paranoia. *S.E., 12:* 1–79.

Freud, S. (1912b). The dynamics of transference. *S.E., 12:* 97–108.

Freud, S. (1912e). Recommendations to physicians practising psychoanalysis. *S.E., 12:* 109–120.

Freud, S. (1912–13). *Totem and Taboo. S.E., 13:* 1–161.

Freud, S. (1914c). On narcissism: an introduction. *S.E., 14:* 67–102.

Freud, S. (1914d). On the history of the psychoanalytic movement. *S.E., 14: 1–66.*

Freud, S. (1914g). Remembering, repeating and working through (Further recommendations on the technique of psycho-analysis, II). *S.E., 12:* 145–156.

Freud, S. (1915a [1914]). Observations on transference-love. *S.E., 12:* 157–171.

Freud, S. (1915e). The unconscious. *S.E., 14:* 159–215.

Freud, S. (1916–17). *Introductory Lectures on Psycho-Analysis. S.E.,* 15–16.

Freud, S. (1917a). A difficulty in the path of psycho-analysis. *S.E., 17:* 135–144.

Freud, S. (1918b [1914]): From the history of an infantile neurosis. *S.E.,* 17: 1–122.

Freud, S. (1919a [1918]). Lines of advance in psycho-analytic therapy. *S.E., 17:* 157–168.

Freud, S. (1920g). *Beyond the Pleasure Principle. S.E., 18:* 1–64.

Freud, S. (1922a). Dreams and telepathy. *S.E., 18:* 195–220.

Freud, S. (1922b). Some neurotic mechanisms in jealousy, paranoia and homosexuality. *S.E., 18:* 221–232.

Freud, S. (1922d). Prize offer. *S.E., 17:* 270.

Freud, S. (1923a). Two encyclopaedia articles. *S.E., 18:* 1–59.

Freud, S. (1923b). *The Ego and the Id. S.E., 19:* 1–59.

Freud, S. (1924d). The dissolution of the Oedipus complex. *S.E., 19:* 171–179.

Freud, S. (1925d [1924]). *An Autobiographical Study. S.E., 20:* 1–70.

Freud, S. (1925h). Negation. *S.E., 19:* 233–239.

Freud, S. (1926d). *Inhibitions, Symptoms and Anxiety. S.E., 20:* 75–174.

Freud, S. (1930a). *Civilization and Its Discontents. S.E.*, 21: 59.

Freud, S. (1930e). Address delivered in the Goethe House at Frankfurt. *S.E.*, 21: 208–212.

Freud, S. (1933a). *New Introductory Lectures on Psycho-Analysis. S.E.*, 22: 1–182.

Freud, S. (1933c). Sándor Ferenczi. *S.E.*, 22: 225–229.

Freud, S. (1937c). Analysis terminable and interminable. *S.E.*, 23: 209–253.

Freud, S. (1939a). *Moses and Monotheism. S.E.*, 23: 1–137.

Freud, S. (1940a [1938]). *An Outline of Psycho-Analysis. S.E.*, 23: 139–207.

Freud, S. (1940e). Splitting of the Ego in the process of defence. *S.E.*, 23: 271–278.

Freud, S. (1941d [1921]). Psycho-analysis and telepathy. *S.E.*, 18: 173–193.

Freud, S. (1955a [1907–08]). Original Record of the Case of Obsessional Neurosis (the "Rat Man"). *S.E.*, 10: 259.

Freud, S. (1960a). *Letters of Sigmund Freud 1873–1939*. London: Hogarth Press; New York: Basic Books.

Freud, S. (1974b). *L'Homme aux Rats. Journal d'une analyse*. Paris: Presses Universitaires de France.

Freud, S. (1989). *The Letters of S. Freud to Ed. Silberstein 1871–1881*. Cambridge, MA: Harvard University Press, 1990.

Freud, S., & Abraham, K. (1965a). *A Psychoanalytic Dialogue. The Letters of Sigmund Freud and Karl Abraham, 1907–1926*. London: Hogarth Press.

Freud, S., & Binswanger, L. (1995). *Correspondance 1908–1938*. Paris: Calmann-Lévy, 1995.

Freud, S., & Ferenczi, S. (1993). *Correspondence, vol. 1, 1908–1914*. Cambridge, MA: Harvard University Press.

Freud, S., & Ferenczi, S. (1996). *Correspondence, vol. 2, 1914–1919*. Cambridge, MA: Harvard University Press.

Freud, S., & Ferenczi, S. (2000). *Correspondence, vol. 3, 1918–1933*. Cambridge, MA: Harvard University Press.

Freud, S., & Jones, E. (1993). *The Complete Correspondence of Sigmund Freud and Ernest Jones 1908–1939*. Cambridge, MA: Harvard University Press.

Freud, S., & Jung. C. G. (1974). *The Freud/Jung Letters*. Princeton, NJ:

Princeton University Press. Reprinted: Cambridge, MA: Harvard University Press, 1988.

Freud, S., & Pfister, O. (1963). *Psychoanalysis and Faith. The Letters of Sigmund Freud and Oskar Pfister, 1909–1939.* London: Hogarth Press/New York: Basic Books.

Fuller, P. (1985). Introduction. In: C. Rycroft, *Psychoanalysis and Beyond.* London: The Hogarth Press, pp. 1–38.

Glover, E. (1927). Lectures on technique in psychoanalysis. *International Journal of Psycho-Analysis, 8*: 311–338.

Groddeck, G. (1974). *The Meaning of Illness. Selected Psychoanalytic Writings, Including His Correspondence with Sigmund Freud.* London: Hogarth Press.

Grosskurth, P. (1986). *Melanie Klein. Her World and Her Work.* New York: Alfred Knopf.

Grubrich-Simitis, I. (1993). *Zurück zu Freuds Texten. Stumme Dokumente sprechen machen.* Frankfurt/M.: Fischer.

Guttman, S. A., et al. (Eds.) (1980). *The Concordance of the Standard Edition of the Complete Psychological Works of Sigmund Freud.* Boston, MA: Hall.

Harmat, P. (1986). *Freud, Ferenczi és a magyarországi pszichoanalizis* (Freud, Ferenczi and Hungarian psychoanalysis). Budapest: Bethlen Gábor. Second edition, 1993. *Freud, Ferenczi und die hungarische psychoanalyse.* Tübingen: Diskord, 1988.

Haynal, A. (1987). *The Technique at Issue. Controversies in Psychoanalysis from Freud and Ferenczi to Michael Balint.* London: Karnac Books, 1991.

Haynal, A. (1992a). Introduction. In: *The Correspondence of Sigmund and Sándor Ferenczi. Vol. 1, 1908–1914* (pp. xvii–xxxv). Cambridge, MA: The Belknap Press/Harvard University Press, 1994.

Haynal, A. (1992b). Un bébé savant? *Le Bloc-Notes de la Psychanalyse, 11*: pp. 141–162.

Haynal, A. (1993). Ferenczi and the origins of psychoanalytic technique. In: L. Aron & A. Harris (Eds.), *The Legacy of Sándor Ferenczi.* Hillsdale, NJ: Analytic Press, pp. 53–74.

Haynal, A. (1997). What correspondence between Freud and Ferenczi? In: P. Mahony, C. Bonomi, & J. Stensson (Eds.), *Behind the Scenes. Freud in Correspondence.* Oslo: Scandinavian University Press, 1997, pp. 111–122.

Heimann, P. (1950). On counter-transference. *International Journal of Psycho-Analysis, 31*: 81–84.

Heller, P. (Ed.) (1992). *Anna Freud's Letters to Eva Rosenfeld.* Madison, CT: International Universities Press.

Hirschmüller, A. (1978). *The Life and Work of Josef Breuer. Physiology and Psychoanalysis.* New York/London: New York Universities Press, 1989.

Jennings, J. L. (1986). The revival of "Dora": Advances in psychoanalytic theory and technique. *Journal of Amer. Psychoanalytic Assn, 34*: 607–635.

Jones, E. (1953). *Sigmund Freud, Life and Work, vol. 1: The Young Freud, 1856–1900.* New York: Basic Books.

Jones, E. (1955). *Sigmund Freud, Life and Work, vol. 2: Years of Maturity, 1901–1919.* New York: Basic Books.

Jones, E. (1957). *Sigmund Freud, Life and Work, vol. 3: The last phase, 1919–1939.* New York: Basic Books.

Jones, E. (1959). *Free Associations. Memories of a Psycho-Analyst.* New York: Basic Books.

József, A. (1956). *Összes versei.* Budapest: Szépirodalmi Könyvkiadó.

Jung, C. G. (1906). Psychoanalyse und Assoziationsexperiment (Diagnostische Assoziationsstudien, 6. Beitrag). *Journal of Psychology & Neurology, 7* (1–2): 1–24 (reprinted in: G.W., vol. 2, pp. 308–337, 1979).

Jung, C. G. (1962). *Memories, Dreams, Reflections.* New York/London: Flamingo, 1983.

Junker, H. (1997). *Unter Uebermenschen: Freud & Ferenczi. Die Geschichte einer Beziehung in Briefen.* Tübingen: Diskord.

Khan, M. M. R. (1963). The concept of the cumulative trauma. In: *The privacy of the Self.* London: Hogarth Press/New York: Int. Univ. Press, 1974.

Klein, M. (1946a). Notes on some schizoid mechanisms. *International Journal of Psycho-Analysis, 27*: 99–110.

Klein, M. (1946b). Projective identification. In: R. D. Hinshelwood, *A Dictionary of Kleinian thought* (pp. 179–208). London: Free Association Books, 1991.

Kohon, G. (1986). *The British School of Psychoanalysis: the Independent Tradition.* London: Free Association Books.

Krafft-Ebing, R. von (1886). *Psychopathia Sexualis. Eine klinisch–forensische Studie.* Stuttgart: Ferdinand Enke.

Lieberman, E. J. (1985). *Acts of Will. The Life and Work of Otto Rank*. New York: The Free Press.

Lipton, S. D. (1977). The advantages of Freud's technique as shown in his analysis of the Rat Man. *International Journal of Psycho-Analysis*, 58: 255–274.

Little, M. (1951). Counter-transference and the patient's response to it. *International Journal of Psycho-Analysis*, 32: 32–40.

Little, M. (1957). "R"—The analyst's total response to his patient's needs. *International Journal of Psycho-Analysis*, 38: 240–254.

Little, M. (1990). *Psychotic Anxieties and Containment, A Personal Record of an Analysis with Winnicott*. London: Jason Aronson.

Lorin, C. (1983). *Le jeune Ferenczi. Premiers écrits, 1899–1906*. Paris: Aubier.

Lorin, C. (1993). *Sándor Ferenczi de la médecine à la psychanalyse*. Paris: Presses Universitaires de France.

Mahony, P. (1993). Psychoanalysis—the writing cure. *Cahiers Psychiatriques Genevois*. Geneva: Médecine et Hygiène. *Special Issue: 100 Years of Psychoanalysis. Contributions to the History of Psychoanalysis* (pp. 101–119). London: Karnac Books.

Mahony, P., Bonomi, C., & Stensson, J. (1997). *Behind the Scenes. Freud in Correspondance*. Stockholm: Scandinavian University Press.

Masson, J. M. (1984). *The Assault on Truth. Freud's Suppression of the Seduction Theory*. New York: Penguin Books.

Masson, J. M. (1985). *The Complete Letters of Sigmund Freud to Wilhelm Fliess 1887–1904*. Cambridge, MA: Belknap.

Mészáros, J. (Ed.) (1999). *Sándor Ferenczi: A pszichoanalizis felé. Fiatalkori irások 1897–1908*. Budapest: Osiris.

Moreau-Ricaud, M. (Ed.) (1992). *Cure d'ennui. Ecrivains hongrois autour de Sándor Ferenczi*. Paris: Gallimard.

Nemes, L., & Berényi, G. (Eds.) (1999). *Die budapester Schule der Psychoanalyse*. Budapest: Akadémia.

Noble, D., & Burnham, D. L. (1969). *History of The Washington Psychoanalytic Society and The Washington Psychoanalytic Institute*. Washington, DC: privately printed, September 1969.

Nunberg, H., & Federn, E. (Eds.) (1962). *Minutes of the Vienna Psychoanalytic Society. Vol. 1, 1906–1908*. New York: International Universities Press.

Paskauskas, R. A. (1988). Freud's break with Jung: the crucial role of Ernest Jones. *Free Associations*, 11: 7–34.

Pfitzner, R. (1999). Das Trauma in der Sicht der Budapester Schule. *Luzifer-Amor*, 12/23: 9–24.

Rachman, A. W. (1993). Ferenczi and sexuality. In: L. Aron & A. Harris (Eds.), *The Legacy of Sándor Ferenczi* (pp. 81–100). Hillsdale, NJ: Analytic Press.

Rachman, A. W. (1997a). *Sándor Ferenczi. The Psychotherapist of Tenderness and Passion*. Northvale, NJ: Jason Aronson.

Rachman, A. W. (Issue Ed.) (1997b). Psychoanalysis' favorite son. The legacy of Sándor Ferenczi. *Psychoanalytic Inquiry*, 17 (4).

Racker, H. (1953). A contribution to the problem of countertransference. *International Journal of Psycho-Analysis*, 34: 313–324.

Racker, H. (1957). The meanings and uses of countertransference. *Psychoanalytic Quarterly*, 26: 303–357.

Rank, O. (1924). *The Trauma of Birth*. London: Kegan Paul and Co., 1929 (rev. ed., New York: Harper & Row, 1973).

Rank, O., & Sachs, H. (1913). *The Significance of Psychoanalysis for the Mental Sciences*. New York: Nervous and Mental Disease Publishing Co., 1916.

Reich, W. (1933). *Character Analysis*. Rangelay, Maine: Oregone Institute Press, 1945.

Roazen, P. (1969). *Brother Animal. The Story of Freud and Tausk*. New York: Vintage Books.

Roazen, P. (1971). *Freud and His Followers*. New York: Alfred A. Knopf.

Roheim, G. (1950). *Psychoanalysis and Anthropology*. New York: International Universities Press.

Rosen, J. N. (1946). Method of resolving acute catatonic excitement. *Psychiatric Quarterly*, 20 (April 1946): 183–198.

Rosen, J. N. (1947). Treatment of schizophrenic psychosis by direct analytic therapy. *Psychiatric Quarterly*, 21 (January 1947): 3–37.

Rosenzweig, S. (1992). *Freud, Jung and Hall the King-Maker: The Historic Expedition to America (1909), with G. Stanley Hall as Host and William James as Guest*. St. Louis/Seattle: Rana House Press, Hogrefe & Huber.

Roustang, F. (1976). *Un destin si funeste*. Paris: Editions de Minuit.

Rudnytsky, P. L., Bókay, A., & Giampieri-Deutsch, P. (Eds.) (1996). *Ferenczi's Turn in Psychoanalysis*. New York: New York University Press.

Ruitenbeek, H. M. (1973). *Freud as We Knew Him*. Detroit, MI: Wayne State University Press.

Sabourin, P. (1985). *Ferenczi, Paladin et Grand Vizir secret*. Paris: Editions Universitaires.

Sharpe, E. (1921). The technique of psychoanalysis, *International Journal of Psycho-Anal*, 2: 361–386.

Stanton, M. (1991). *Sándor Ferenczi. Reconsidering Active Intervention*. Northvale, NJ: Jason Aronson.

Taft, J. (1958). *Otto Rank*. New York: The Julian Press.

Thompson, C. (1944). Ferenczi's contribution to psychoanalysis. *Psychiatry*, 7: 245–252.

Thompson, C. (1955). In: D. Noble & D. L. Burnham (1969). *History of The Washington Psychoanalytic Society and The Washington Psychoanalytic Institute*. Washington, DC: privately printed, September 1969.

Thompson, C. (1956). The rôle of the analyst's personality in therapy. *American Journal of Psychotherapy*, 10: 347–359.

Vida, J. (1996). Sándor Ferenczi: amalgamating with the existing body of knowledge. *Cahiers Psychiatriques Genevois, Special Issue: 100 Years of Psychoanalysis. Contributions to the History of Psychoanalysis* (pp. 257–263). Geneva: Médecine et Hygiène. London: Karnac Books.

Vikár, G. (1999a). Die Problematik der Aggression in der Auffassung von Imre Hermann und der "Budapester Schule". *Luzifer-Amor*, 12 (23): 84–96.

Vikár, G. (1999b). Die Motive des Leidens und des Todes. *Luzifer-Amor*, 12/23: 175–181.

Wallerstein, R. S. (1988). One psychoanalysis or many? *International Journal of Psycho-Analysis*, 69: 5–22.

Williams, P. (1999). "Non-interpretative mechanisms in psychoanalytic therapy", by Daniel Stern et al., and "What is 'applied' in 'applied' psychoanalysis?", by Aaron H. Esman. *International Journal of Psycho-Analysis*, 80: 197–210.

Winnicott, D. W. (1947). Hate in the counter-transference. *International Journal of Psycho-Analysis*, 30: 69–74.

Wolstein, B. (1989). Ferenczi, Freud, and the origins of American interpersonal relations. *Contemporary Psychoanalysis*, 25: 672–685.

Young-Bruehl, E. (1988). *Anna Freud, A Biography*. New York: Summit Books, 1990.

Zweig, S. (1989). *Über Sigmund Freud—Porträt, Briefwechsel, Gedenkworte*. Frankfurt/M.: Fischer.

INDEX

elasticity, 49
empathy vs. insight, 39
"epistemological discontinuity", 13
Eros, 9, 51
Erös, F., 94
erotomania, analyst's, 67–68
Erzsébet Szegényház, 3
experience [*Erlebnis*], analytic, 32, 46,
    50, 63, 65, 68, 71, 73, 79, 80, 84
    vs. insight, 39
experimentation, 25
    in therapeutic situation, 11–12

Fairbairn, W. R. D., 126
false self, 47, 126
Falzeder, E., xii, 120, 126
Federn, E., 7, 20, 24, 33, 78, 85
Fenichel, O., 69, 98
Ferenczi, B., 1
Ferenczi, G. (Pálos, née Altschul), 11,
    18, 20–22, 81–83, 92, 95, 96, 99,
    116
Ferenczi, S., *passim*
    affair with Elma Pálos, 11, 18, 20–
        23, 56, 77, 82–84, 86, 92, 95–97,
        116
    Clinical Diary, 3, 10, 11, 16, 17, 19,
        25, 39–42, 49–50, 58–61, 66, 68,
        77, 105, 108, 122, 129
    as dissident, 101–109
    "Dm." (Clara Thompson) case, 57–
        58, 66, 89, 108, 122, 128, 129
    experimentation of, in therapeutic
        situation, 11–12
    family history, 1–3
    and Freud, *passim*
    interest in childhood, 10–11
    interest in occultism, 3–9
    interest in sexuality, 9–10
    and Jones, 120
    "little Árpád", 11
    "N.G." case, 58
    as "pre"-psychoanalyst, 1–14
    R.N. [Elisabeth Severn: "Orpha"]
        case, 40, 41, 50, 60–62, 65–66,
        119
    "Thalassa", 9, 26, 48, 52
Ferenczi, V., 66

Fischer, D., 24
Fliess, W., xiii, 4, 11, 43, 76, 103–105,
    113–114, 121
Fluss, G., 76
Forel, A., 77
Foucault, M., 70
Fraenkel, B., 1
fragmentation:
    of individuality, 60
    of personality, 39, 48
free association, 4, 5, 27, 85
Freud, A., 4, 6, 11, 18, 20, 34, 80, 84,
    89, 120, 122, 126, 127
Freud, E., 92
Freud, M., 18, 34, 93
Freud Museum, London, 35
Freud, S., *passim*
    "Dora" (I. Bauer) case, 7, 41, 75–76
    and Ferenczi, *passim*
    Itzig story, 16
    "Rat Man" case, 8, 33, 78, 86
    Schreber case, 18, 113–116
    self-analysis of, 4
    "Wolf Man" case, 108, 122
Frink, H. W., 128
Fromm, E., 128
Fuller, P., 126

Gedo, J., 89
genitality, theory of, Ferenczi's, 68
Giampieri, P., 94
Glover, E., 57
Goethe, J. W. von, 9, 70, 116
gratification, erotic, in treatment, 97
Graven, P., 129
Groddeck, G., xiii, 11, 16, 20, 26, 60,
    86, 109, 114, 117
    and Ferenczi, 87, 93, 117
    and Freud, 18, 92, 117
Gross, O., 20, 60
Grosskurth, P., 56
Grubrich-Simitis, I., 4
Guex, G., 45
Guntrip, H., 126
Guttman, S. A., 103

Habsburg, House of, 2
Hartmann, E. von, 98

148   INDEX